George Foreman's
Big George Rotisserie Cookbook

GEORGE FOREMAN'S

Big George Rotisserie Cookbook

written by

GEORGE FOREMAN & CONNIE MERYDITH

Pascoe Publishing

Cover design by Mary Beth Salmon
Page design by Melanie Haage
Editing by Heidi J. Purvis
Nutritional Analyses by Energy Enterprises

ISBN 1-929862-00-8

99 00 01 02 03 10 9 8 7 6 5 4 3 2 1

Printed in the United States of America

Dedication

I dedicate this book to the memory of my Mom, Nancy Foreman, who taught us that anyone can cook, but it takes a special love of family to make certain that every meal is prepared with heart and soul. It is that touch of love that makes one say, "That was *so* good. Thank you!"

—George Foreman

This book is dedicated to my Mom and Dad, who sat at the table with my sisters and me after dinner every night and turned some of the most simple meals into truly memorable, loving experiences.

—Connie Merydith

Acknowledgments

We would like to extend our thanks and appreciation to people who helped create this cookbook:

To Heidi Jo Purvis, our editor, who took a rough manuscript and polished it with a keen eye and a good sense of humor.

We appreciate the efforts of nutritionist Jinny Elder at Energy Enterprises, who consulted with us to create healthful recipes and who spent many hours analyzing the nutritional contents of each one.

And, finally, our warmest thanks to Tom Strong, who prepared ingredients, tested recipes, offered suggestions and even cleaned up the kitchen afterward. You made it fun.

Table of Contents

Preface

One of the most important elements of my life is eating the right kinds of food. When I was a child growing up, my family was poor and sometimes there wasn't enough food to go around. I know that my mother did everything she could to provide myself and my six brothers and sisters with healthy foods, but I was constantly looking forward to the next meal. I just couldn't seem to get enough. As a young teenager, I especially enjoyed spending what little money I had on thick cheeseburgers with all the trimmings. That was the ultimate treat! I grew to be six feet, four inches and strengthened my frame by training for my boxing career. And, during the next several years, I continued to eat without giving any thought about the types of food I chose. If something tasted good, I ate it! Then, after ten years of retirement from professional boxing, I decided to return to the ring.

When I first made the choice to return to professional boxing, I knew I wanted to achieve two things. I wanted to return with a new attitude and outlook on life, and I wanted to return in the best physical shape possible. I started by taking a good, hard look at my out-of-shape body and the foods I was eating. I began to recognize that not every food I enjoyed was good for me. In fact, I realized that a large percentage of what I ate was loaded with fat and calories and was doing me more harm than good. So, I started by choosing fresh vegetables and fruit more often. At dinnertime, I chose fish, chicken, turkey and lean cuts of meat. I tried to watch for ways to get the fat out of my everyday diet. My meals didn't have to be fancy or complicated; they simply had to be a healthful balance of the foods I knew I needed. And, I'm happy to say, when I learned to eat foods that contribute to a healthy life, I met my personal goals of achievement and once again entered the boxing ring to become a champion.

Today, I still enjoy food and I know I always will. And, of course, I still carefully watch the foods that I eat. When the *George Foreman Lean Mean Fat Reducing Grilling Machine* was introduced a few years ago, I was delighted to find that poultry, fish and red meats prepared in the grill were tender, flavorful and had less fat because of the grill's unique design. And, it was exciting to watch as hundreds of thousands of people discovered the same thing for themselves. Now, with the new *George Foreman Lean Mean Fat Reducing Roasting Machine*, I'm learning just how versatile this rotisserie oven can be! Whether you choose to rotisserie a chicken or serve up a platter of fat-free, air-baked potatoes, you'll find plenty of choices to help you maintain your healthy lifestyle. I hope you enjoy these recipes and find new ways to knock out the fat every day. After all, in the big picture of life, that's what being a champion is all about!

—George Foreman

Introduction

Welcome to the exciting world of rotisserie cooking! If you have never used a rotisserie before, you'll soon discover why this method of cooking is preferred all over the world. The recipes in this cookbook have been designed to accompany your Big George rotisserie and the special features it offers. And, as co-authors, we've combined our skills and favorite foods to give you a wide variety of healthy, lowfat food choices. For example, George particularly enjoys lean meat, poultry, fresh fruit and vegetables, so you'll find a good selection of recipes using each in the following chapters. Connie likes to combine lowfat foods to create healthy appetizers, pasta dishes, snacks and desserts. We hope that, as you use your Big George rotisserie and the recipes we've created, you'll find recipes that become your favorites, as well.

How does your rotisserie work? The basic idea behind the rotisserie is that as the meat cooks the fat drips down and away, eliminating much of the fat that would normally accumulate. Also, as the rotisserie turns, meat juices sear the outside, sealing in the flavor and tenderness of the meat. The end result? Tender and moist meats, poultry and fish without all the heavy fat!

What are the special features of your rotisserie? Your rotisserie really *is* the ultimate in rotisserie ovens. It has unique accessories such as the Roasted

Veggie/Air Bake Basket, which allows you to air-bake lowfat vegetables with delicious results. Your rotisserie includes the Baking Sheet and the Wire Rack which can be used for baking muffins, cakes and breads. And it includes convenience items such as a selection of Meat Tines and the Rotisserie Bar Remover. This cookbook was designed to be your partner to put all these outstanding features to work for you and your family. You'll discover recipes for delicious and tender meats, poultry and fish. You will find a large selection of lowfat accompaniments, salads, vegetables and tempting desserts. And, best of all, these recipes have been created with your good health in mind. So, what are you waiting for? Let's get started!

■ ■ ■

A NOTE TO THE COOK

In each chapter of this book you'll find notes and tips in sections titled "A Note to the Cook," to help you plan and prepare your rotisserie foods. Whether you are a complete novice to rotisserie cooking or a veteran of many years, it's always important to start with the basics, so read your Owner's Manual completely and take a few minutes to check out the safety tips outlined below.

■ Read the Owner's Manual instructions for the proper use of your rotisserie and for all assembly instructions.

■ Be very careful of potentially hot surfaces and the heating elements. Use mitts and hot pads when removing cooked foods.

■ Don't try to fit oversized foods into the oven.

- To avoid the risk of shock, use plastic utensils whenever possible.

- When using a meat thermometer do not try to test the meat while it is still in the oven. Remove the meat first and then test.

- Pour a small amount of water into the Drip Tray when using your rotisserie for meats and poultry. This will help eliminate smoke that can be caused by dripping fat.

- Be very cautious when you are removing the Drip Tray containing hot grease. Pour the hot grease into an empty aluminum can or other sturdy container and let it cool. When the grease is completely cool, wrap the used can in a self-sealing plastic bag and dispose. Don't pour grease down the sink, as it may clog the drains.

- Use sanitary cutting boards and clean them thoroughly after use. Because bacteria growth can cause cross-contamination of foods, don't use the same cutting board for meats and other foods. Keep at least two or three clean cutting boards available for every meal.

- Many of these recipes call for diced or sliced foods. Use the appropriate knife for each task and use an extra measure of caution when you are handling sharp knives.

- It's best to dispose of a marinade after using it with raw meat, fish or poultry rather than using it as a sauce with the cooked meat. If you do want to use it as a sauce, boil the marinade for at least 5 minutes first to kill the bacteria that may have accumulated.

- *Always* keep foods in the refrigerator while marinating. Different strains of bacteria love warm temperatures, so keep raw meats and foods cold until you intend to use them. Leftovers should be promptly refrigerated, as well.

- The recipes in this book offer a suggested length of time for proper cooking. You may want to watch and make adjustments to suit your own tastes, or to accommodate a variance in the weight or thickness of the meat. If you're in doubt about the correct cooking time, set the Timer for a shorter cycle and check the progress accordingly. It's better to test the meat a few times than to overcook it.

Chapter 1

What Have You Got to Gain When You Knock Out the Fat?

Here's the bad news—approximately one-third of the people in our country are overweight and, as a result, are unhealthy. Common conditions related to obesity such as diabetes, high blood pressure and heart disease play an enormous part in our medical costs. The drugs and programs that are required to treat these conditions cost this nation *billions* of dollars every year. So, armed with that bite of reality, let's talk about you for a minute. Why is it important to *you* to knock out the fat? What do you want to *achieve* by eating less fat? Take a minute to write down your goals for health and weight management. Think about what you have to *gain* by eating healthy foods. What do you want to look like and how do you want to feel in three months, six months and a year? Once you've outlined your own goals, put them where you can see them everyday. And, now, because you know *why* you want to knock out the fat, let's talk about just exactly *how* to do it.

■ ■ ■

FAT: WHO NEEDS IT?

Let's start talking about fat with the knowledge that we all need *some* fat in our diets. About 10% of the average adult's total calories each day should come from fat. Infants and children need more fat simply because their bodies require it for proper growth. If, as popular research tells us, women should consume around 1,500 calories a day and men should consume about 2,000 calories a day, that means our fat should be no more than 15 grams per day for women and 20 grams per day for men. These amounts will vary with the size and gender of individuals. However, as appropriate as these suggested fat percentages may seem, the sad truth is that most of us consume far more fat every day than we should. In fact, any one individual food item you eat during the day can push those fat grams through the roof before you are even aware of it. All it takes is a buttery breakfast pastry, one beefy hamburger or a thick milkshake and your fat gram count will soar out of control. So, start your healthy eating plan by knowing how many fat grams you should be consuming and then watch and count those grams during a typical day. Buy a small pocket book that lists the fat grams of typical foods. Try to gauge how many fat grams you are eating by writing down *every single food* you put in your mouth for one week. Armed with this knowledge, you can start to knock out the fat by preparing and eating foods low in fat every day. This may seem tedious at first, but again, think about what you have to *gain* by knocking out the fat.

■ ■ ■

20 QUICK WAYS TO KNOCK OUT THE FAT:

- Watch that fat! Watch out for foods prepared with butter and margarine, oil, mayonnaise, salad dressings, cheese and cream. Don't let those "hidden" fats exist in your daily diet.

- Make substitutions for fat. Use fresh juices, fat-free and lowfat margarine, mayonnaise and dressings. Use spices and herbs to accent dishes that typically call for heavy fats. You don't have to sacrifice delicious flavors to eat a lowfat meal.

- Use methods of cooking that reduce the natural fat found in foods. Use your rotisserie to drain much of the fat from the meat, poultry and fish you prepare. Avoid frying foods unless you use non-stick cooking spray and a non-stick pan.

- Try new lowfat foods from your supermarket. Look for lowfat turkey bacon, lunchmeats, cheeses, yogurt, soups and snack items. You'll find new lowfat foods almost every time you shop. Look at the labels carefully to determine how many servings are indicated, the portion size and the total fat grams. The fat gram count for roasted peanuts may not seem very high until you realize that one serving size may be only three or four nuts. Most of us could easily eat twenty in one handful!

- Stock up on fresh vegetables and fruits and *eat* them. It's easy to buy good-for-you foods with the best of intentions and it's also easy to ignore them once you've taken them home. The next time you reach for a snack, reach for fresh vegetables or chilled fruit.

You'll gain healthy and younger-looking skin, better digestion and more energy by making the choice to eat fruits and vegetables.

- Take a walk around the block. Ride your bike. Jump a rope. Include exercise in your day to boost your metabolism and burn that fat. This may not be, in reality, an "easy tip" for you to adopt if you dislike exercising, but remember what you have to *gain* by doing it. Start slowly, if necessary, and build up to a daily exercise routine. You must exercise your muscles to reach your goal of good health.

- Watch those calories! Just because a food is lowfat, doesn't necessarily mean you won't be eating calories. Every food item counts in your eating plan. When making your choices, remember that high-carbohydrate foods such as potatoes, whole-grain breads and pasta contribute much more nutritive value to your day than non-nutritive foods such as sodas or surgery snacks.

- Make sure you snack. Yes, that's right! You should snack to keep extreme hunger from allowing you to make poor choices at mealtimes. A healthy snack at mid-morning and mid-afternoon will help you to concentrate during the day and provide you with stable energy levels all day. Carry a few healthy snacks with you, if possible, to avoid the urge to buy high-fat snacks. Opt for a small bag of toasted soybeans, pretzels, or a handful of raisins instead.

- Make sure you prepare foods for optimum nutrients and flavor. Many of us overcook our foods to the point that they lose nutrients and flavor. If your cooked vegetables are mushy, you can be sure that you've cooked away the major portion of vitamins and minerals. The combination of heat and water reduces the vitamins and minerals found naturally in our foods, so eat raw foods when possible. Some foods such as meats must be cooked to destroy bacteria, but remember to preserve as much flavor as possible by not overcooking.

■ Use portion control to lose the fat in your diet. For example, most of us believe that a "small" steak is around six ounces. According to the U.S. Department of Agriculture, one appropriate serving of steak is around 3 ounces. Try to reduce the size of your servings of fat. Use one teaspoon of margarine instead of three. Take one spoonful of salad dressing instead of two.

■ Slow down. Take time to eat your meals. Savor your foods. It takes your brain about 30 minutes to tell your stomach that you're full, and you'll digest your foods better if you eat slowly, so take it easy. Don't eat your meals standing up or in your car. You won't feel as if you've *really* eaten a meal and you won't feel as relaxed afterward.

■ Serve sauces on the side. Let everyone choose their own amount and try to watch your own portions carefully. Most prepared and restaurant sauces are loaded with fat.

■ Eating out can be problematic unless you're prepared before you walk through the door. First, try to eat a small healthy snack before you go, so you won't be tempted by the high-fat choices. Second, look for foods that are naturally lower in fat such as green salads (with no dressing or the dressing on the side) broiled fish or chicken and plain baked potatoes. If you want to include dessert, opt for fruit or a scoop of nonfat frozen yogurt. If you are tempted, remind yourself why you are making lowfat choices and what you have to gain.

- Don't be shy about making requests for specially prepared foods when you dine out. You may want to request poultry or fish without sauce, or pasta without grated cheese on top, and most restaurants are happy to accommodate such requests.

- Nonfat frozen yogurt is a nice treat once in a while and contains calcium for strong bones. Don't forget, however, to avoid the toppings such as nuts and candy. Try fresh fruit for your topping instead.

- Late-night snacking can quickly destroy your goals for good health. In fact, research tells us that it's best to eat the majority of our foods early in the day and let our stomachs rest in the evening. So, it's best to simply avoid eating anything at all after dinner, but, if you must snack, make sure it is a nonfat food. Also, keep your portions small enough so that your body can digest the food while you sleep.

- If you travel as part of your job, prepare healthy foods for your day and pack a small cooler before you get in the car. If you're not able to prepare foods each day, drive to the supermarket at lunchtime and buy lowfat foods to make your lunch. Try sliced lowfat turkey, lowfat granola bars, fruit, nonfat milk and pretzels. If fast food is your only choice, buy turkey sandwiches with no mayonnaise or oil, plain, baked potatoes or broiled chicken sandwiches with no dressing.

- Tell your family and friends that you are making changes in your eating plan. By doing this, you will be able to enlist their help and understanding when you implement these changes.

- Make one change every week to move toward better health. It doesn't have to be a drastic change, but take small, steady steps and each will lead you to becoming the healthy person you really want to be.

- BE DETERMINED. Remind yourself at least twice a day of your personal goals toward better health. Don't give up the determination to change your eating habits. And, even if you still have an occasional "high-fat day," don't lose sight of what you'll gain by knocking out the fat. Get back to your lowfat plan the next day. True changes in our eating patterns aren't instantaneous, nor are they always easy. But, by adopting these eating suggestions, you will see and feel the results of knocking out that fat—and you will have gained a healthier life!

A HEALTHY BALANCE: HOW TO FIND IT . . . AND WHAT TO DO WITH IT WHEN YOU GET IT

If you chose to empty your pantry shelves and restock them with only lowfat foods, and then you ate only those lowfat foods, you would automatically become a healthy person, right? Wrong! At first glance, it's easy to assume that all you have to do to lose weight and become healthy is avoid fats and then you can eat everything else. Does this mean that you can eat fifteen boxes of sugarcoated, fat-free popcorn in one day and you'll be healthy? Not likely. Or, according one popular diet, if we avoid carbohydrates and eat everything else we'll be healthy. Does this mean we can eat eight or nine porterhouse steaks in one day and be healthy? Doubtful. What about the diet that tells us to simply avoid all sugars and eat everything else? Are you confused? Join the rest of us. Because, the truth is, despite all of the popular diets, we need to put a *balance* of healthy foods into our bodies in order for our bodies to truly be healthy. *That's* the real goal of weight management. If you've been happily munching away all day on lowfat cookies and chips and you can't understand why you haven't lost weight, consider the fact that foods need to be eaten with a healthy perspective.

According to the U.S. Department of Agriculture, there are some foods we should eat *every day* in order to achieve and maintain a healthy balance in our diet:

- **Bread, Cereal, Rice and Pasta:** Eat 6–11 servings daily. A serving is 1 slice of bread, ½ cup cooked cereal or ½ cup of cooked rice or pasta.

- **Vegetables:** Eat 3–5 servings daily. A serving is ½ cup chopped raw or cooked vegetables, 1 cup of leafy vegetables or ¾ cup of vegetable juice.

- **Fruits:** Eat 2–4 servings daily. A serving is one piece of fruit, ¾ cup of fruit juice or ½ cup of canned fruit.

- **Dairy Foods (Milk, Yogurt, and Cheese):** Eat 2–3 servings daily. A serving is 1 cup of milk, 1 cup of yogurt or 1–2 ounces of cheese.

- **Meat, Poultry, Fish, Beans & Lentils, Eggs & Nuts:** Eat 2–3 servings daily. A serving is 2½–3 ounces of cooked meat, poultry or fish, ½ cup of cooked beans or lentils, 1 egg or a small handful of nuts.

■ **Fats, Oils and Sweets:** Use Sparingly. There are no recommendations for how much of these items you should eat simply because they should be the *least* of all the components of your daily diet. Typically, a single serving is about one tablespoon of butter or oil or four tablespoons of sugar.

■ ■ ■

After taking a quick look at these recommendations, you'll know why fad diets that completely omit certain foods probably won't lead you to better health. Following the guidelines above *will* promote you to better health and you'll lose excess weight along the way. A good way to start using these suggested servings is to record your eating for a week and then place each of your food choices within the group where it belongs. Total up your servings for each day and determine whether or not you are eating a healthy balance of foods. Then, look at your fat grams again and take away what you don't really need. Look at your calorie intake and shave off unnecessary calories. Follow a steady routine of eating the right foods and you will achieve your goals—you will *gain* the good health you deserve.

A NOTE ABOUT NUTRITIONAL ANALYSES

Each of the recipes in this book is accompanied by a nutritional analysis designed to help you calculate fat, calories and other helpful information. Use these analyses to guide your food choices for each meal. The nutritional analyses are based on typical serving sizes and optional ingredients have not been included. When a recipe specifies "lowfat" or "fat-free" ingredients, the nutritional analysis is based on that type of ingredient.

Chapter 2

Sauces, Rubs & Marinades: The Spice of Life

Just as we all like to vary our daily routines, we also like to explore and taste new flavors. If you stop to think about it, you may realize that today's popular spices and flavors are quite different from those we used even a decade ago. And, the flavors most popular ten years ago were different from those of the previous decade. And, so on, back to centuries ago, when spices were used as much to help preserve meats from spoilage as they were to create new and exotic taste sensations for ancient royalty. Today's spices and flavors such as chili, lime, hoisin, cilantro and ginger inspire us to exchange our everyday recipes for fresh, new ones. So, take time to explore the recipes in this chapter and enjoy sauces, rubs and marinades—just for a change.

A NOTE TO THE COOK

Sauces, rubs and marinades are *really* fun. They are fun to prepare, because they take very little time, and they are fun to serve, because the spices and the rotisserie process combine to produce a truly lovely entrée for your meal. The truth is, with your rotisserie, a roast or chicken and a handful of spices;

you're practically done with your meal preparation. And, with our busy lives, that's the way it should be! Here are a few tips you will want to keep in mind as you prepare sauces, rubs and marinades.

- Sauces are best served on the side so that everyone can control their own portion size.

- Rubs, which are spices mixed together and pressed into the meat before roasting, are super easy because there is no marinating time required. Simply rub and roast.

- Marinades are a blend of spices, juice, vinegar and oils. Meat, poultry and fish are usually marinated for several hours, to allow the flavors of the marinade to partially infuse the meat. This creates a more tender and flavorful piece of meat.

- One of the best ways to marinate meat is to use a large, sealable plastic bag. Measure the marinade ingredients into the bag, place the meat in the bag, seal it and smooth the marinade all over the meat. When you're ready to rotisserie, throw away the bag and you're done!

- For best results, turn the meat in the marinade occasionally during the marinating process. This will help give an even flavor and distribution of spices.

- Don't use an aluminum bowl for marinating. The aluminum may react to the acid in the marinade, which will stain the bowl. Also, the aluminum may alter the flavor of the marinade itself. Use a glass or stainless steel bowl instead.

- To make a lowfat marinade, carefully control the amount of oil you use. In some recipes, you may substitute juice, water or a small amount of vinegar for the oil.

- It's safest to discard a marinade after using it on raw meat, poultry or fish. If, however, you want to use it as a sauce for the cooked meat, you should boil it for at least 5 minutes to remove possible bacteria.

1 MARINADES: A TASTE FOR ALL SEASONS

Marinades actually go to work on meat, poultry and fish by tenderizing as they add flavor. Although a marinade won't typically infuse the entire piece of meat, it helps make a naturally lean cut of meat, poultry or fish more tender and moist. That's great news for those of us who want to knock out the fat!

Ginger & Garlic Marinade
For fish and poultry.

1 c.	rice wine vinegar
1 T.	sesame oil
1 T.	minced fresh ginger
2 T.	minced garlic
2 T.	soy sauce
1 t.	five-spice powder

NUTRITIONAL ANALYSIS	
Calories:	7
Total fat:	<1 g
Saturated fat:	<1 g
% calories fat:	74
Carbohydrates:	0 g
Protein:	0 g
Cholesterol:	0 mg
Sodium:	92 mg

Mix together the ingredients and pour into a plastic container. Cover tightly and refrigerate up to one week. Makes 1½ cups.

Lime Marinade

Especially for fish.

1 T.	olive oil
1 c.	fresh lime juice
2 T.	minced garlic
1 t.	thyme
1 t.	marjoram
$1/2$ t.	pepper

NUTRITIONAL ANALYSIS	
Calories:	10
Total fat:	<1 g
Saturated fat:	<1 g
% calories fat:	53
Carbohydrates:	2 g
Protein:	0 g
Cholesterol:	0 mg
Sodium:	0 mg

Whisk the ingredients together and pour into a plastic container. Cover tightly and refrigerate up to one week. Makes 1½ cups.

Tangy Apple Marinade

For beef or poultry.

1 c.	unsweetened apple juice
1 T.	minced garlic
2 t.	dry mustard
2 t.	sesame oil
$1/4$ c.	soy sauce

NUTRITIONAL ANALYSIS	
Calories:	11
Total fat:	<1 g
Saturated fat:	<1 g
% calories fat:	38
Carbohydrates:	2 g
Protein:	0 g
Cholesterol:	0 mg
Sodium:	168 mg

Mix the ingredients together and pour into a plastic container. Cover tightly and refrigerate up to one week. Makes 1½ cups.

Garlic Mustard Marinade
Best with beef.

1 c.	nonfat beef broth
1/2 c.	red wine vinegar
1/2 t.	pepper
2 T.	minced parsley
1 T.	sugar
3 T.	minced garlic
2 T.	olive oil
2 T.	Dijon mustard

NUTRITIONAL ANALYSIS	
Calories:	12
Total fat:	<1 g
Saturated fat:	<1 g
% calories fat:	63
Carbohydrates:	0 g
Protein:	<1 g
Cholesterol:	0 mg
Sodium:	45 mg

Whisk the ingredients together and pour into a plastic container. Cover tightly and refrigerate up to one week. Makes 2 cups.

Sicilian Chicken Marinade
Best with chicken or game hen.

2 T.	olive oil
1/2 c.	fresh lemon juice
1/4 c.	balsamic vinegar
1 T.	chopped fresh basil
1 t.	dried oregano

NUTRITIONAL ANALYSIS	
Calories:	23
Total fat:	2 g
Saturated fat:	<1 g
% calories fat:	67
Carbohydrates:	2 g
Protein:	<1 g
Cholesterol:	0 mg
Sodium:	<1 mg

Mix the ingredients together and pour into a plastic container. Cover tightly and refrigerate up to one week. Makes 1 cup.

Spicy Beef Marinade

Especially good with a large roast.

1 T.	minced garlic
1 T.	pepper
1 T.	chopped onion
1/2 c.	cider vinegar
1/2 c.	ketchup
1/2 c.	Worcestershire sauce

Mix the ingredients together and pour into a plastic container. Cover tightly and refrigerate up to one week. Makes 1½ cups.

NUTRITIONAL ANALYSIS

Calories:	9
Total fat:	<1 g
Saturated fat:	0 g
% calories fat:	2
Carbohydrates:	2 g
Protein:	<1 g
Cholesterol:	0 mg
Sodium:	97 mg

Honey Mustard Marinade

Best with pork or chicken.

1/4 c.	honey
3 T.	yellow mustard
1/2 c.	soy sauce
2 T.	chopped green onion
2 T.	cider vinegar
1 T.	vegetable oil

Mix the ingredients together and pour into a plastic container. Cover tightly and refrigerate up to one week. Makes ¾ cup.

NUTRITIONAL ANALYSIS

Calories:	25
Total fat:	<1 g
Saturated fat:	<1 g
% calories fat:	18
Carbohydrates:	6 g
Protein:	<1 g
Cholesterol:	0 mg
Sodium:	296 mg

Black Pepper Marinade

For beef.

1 t.	pepper
¹/₂ c.	soy sauce
2 T.	sugar
2 T.	minced garlic
¹/₄ c.	red wine vinegar
2 c.	nonfat beef broth

Mix the ingredients together and pour into a plastic container. This can be used as a marinade or a basting sauce for the beef as it cooks. Use immediately or refrigerate up to one week. Makes 2½ cups.

NUTRITIONAL ANALYSIS

Calories:	9
Total fat:	0 g
Saturated fat:	0 g
% calories fat:	0
Carbohydrates:	2 g
Protein:	<1 g
Cholesterol:	0 mg
Sodium:	153 mg

Spicy Orange Marinade

For poultry or pork.

¹/₂ c.	cider vinegar
1 c.	orange juice
2 T.	vegetable oil
1 T.	brown sugar
2 T.	paprika
1 T.	minced garlic

Mix the ingredients together and pour into a plastic container. Cover tightly and refrigerate up to one week. Makes about 1 cup.

NUTRITIONAL ANALYSIS

Calories:	17
Total fat:	1 g
Saturated fat:	<1 g
% calories fat:	48
Carbohydrates:	2 g
Protein:	<1 g
Cholesterol:	0 mg
Sodium:	<1 mg

Hot & Wild Marinade

For beef or poultry.

1 t.	liquid hot sauce (use more or less, as desired)
2 T.	minced garlic
1 T.	brown sugar
2 T.	lime juice
1/2 t.	pepper
1/2 c.	water
1/2 c.	soy sauce

NUTRITIONAL ANALYSIS	
Calories:	6
Total fat:	<1 g
Saturated fat:	0 g
% calories fat:	2
Carbohydrates:	1 g
Protein:	1 g
Cholesterol:	0 mg
Sodium:	360 mg

Whisk the ingredients together and pour into a plastic container. Cover tightly and refrigerate up to one week. Makes 1½ cups.

Oriental Marinade

Perfect for fish.

2 T.	peanut oil
1/4 c.	rice wine vinegar
1/2 c.	soy sauce
1 t.	hot chili sauce
3 T.	minced garlic
1 T.	minced ginger
1 T.	minced cilantro
1 t.	dry mustard

NUTRITIONAL ANALYSIS	
Calories:	18
Total fat:	2 g
Saturated fat:	<1 g
% calories fat:	69
Carbohydrates:	<1 g
Protein:	<1 g
Cholesterol:	0 mg
Sodium:	413 mg

Whisk the ingredients together and pour into a plastic container. Cover tightly and refrigerate up to one week. Makes about 1 cup.

Country Barbecue Marinade

For poultry, pork or lamb.

1/2 c.	unsweetened white grape juice
1/4 c.	minced onion
1 t.	lemon pepper
2 T.	minced garlic
1/4 c.	soy sauce
1 t.	sugar
2 T.	olive oil
1 c.	tomato sauce

NUTRITIONAL ANALYSIS	
Calories:	14
Total fat:	<1 g
Saturated fat:	0 g
% calories fat:	74
Carbohydrates:	1 g
Protein:	<1 g
Cholesterol:	0 mg
Sodium:	187 mg

Mix the ingredients together and pour into a plastic container. Cover tightly and refrigerate up to one week. Makes 2½ cups.

Asian Apple Marinade

Best with pork or poultry.

1 T.	minced parsley
1/4 c.	chopped green onion
1/4 c.	honey
1/2 c.	cider vinegar
1 c.	unsweetened apple juice
1 T.	vegetable oil
2 T.	Worcestershire sauce
1 t.	salt
1/2 t.	pepper

NUTRITIONAL ANALYSIS

Calories:	14
Total fat:	<1 g
Saturated fat:	0 g
% calories fat:	21
Carbohydrates:	3 g
Protein:	0 g
Cholesterol:	0 mg
Sodium:	70 mg

Mix all ingredients in a small saucepan. Bring to a boil and simmer for 15 minutes to dissolve the honey. Use immediately or refrigerate up to one week. Makes 2¼ cups.

Herb Marinade

For any cut of meat, fish or poultry.

2 T.	olive oil
1/2 c.	fresh lemon juice
3 T.	minced garlic
1/2 t.	salt
1/2 t.	pepper
1/2 t.	dried basil

Mix the ingredients together and pour into a plastic container. Cover tightly and refrigerate up to one week. Makes ¾ cup.

NUTRITIONAL ANALYSIS	
Calories:	23
Total fat:	2 g
Saturated fat:	<1 g
% calories fat:	78
Carbohydrates:	1 g
Protein:	<1 g
Cholesterol:	0 mg
Sodium:	181 mg

Lemon & Herb Marinade

For fish, poultry or pork.

1/2 c.	fat-free chicken broth
1/4 c.	fresh lemon juice
2 T.	olive oil
2 T.	minced onion
2 T.	minced garlic
2 t.	dried oregano
1/2 t.	dried rosemary
1/2 t.	salt
1/2 t.	pepper

NUTRITIONAL ANALYSIS	
Calories:	19
Total fat:	2 g
Saturated fat:	<1 g
% calories fat:	74
Carbohydrates:	1 g
Protein:	<1 g
Cholesterol:	0 mg
Sodium:	74 mg

Mix the ingredients together and pour into a plastic container. Cover tightly and refrigerate up to one week. Makes 1 cup.

Smoky Beef Marinade

For large beef roasts.

1 c.	soy sauce
1/2 c.	cider vinegar
2 T.	liquid smoke
1/4 c.	honey
3/4 c.	orange juice
1 T.	red pepper flakes

Mix the ingredients together and pour into a plastic container. Cover tightly and refrigerate up to one week. Makes 2½ cups.

NUTRITIONAL ANALYSIS	
Calories:	10
Total fat:	<1 g
Saturated fat:	<1 g
% calories fat:	2
Carbohydrates:	2 g
Protein:	<1 g
Cholesterol:	0 mg
Sodium:	324 mg

② RUBS: QUICK & EASY

After you've tried these recipes, take another look inside your pantry. You probably have all the ingredients for your own special rub recipe!

Big Cajun Rub

For beef or pork.

2 T.	dried minced onion
1 t.	dried thyme
½ t.	salt
2 t.	chili powder
1 t.	garlic powder

Mix the ingredients together. Store the rub in a plastic container or bag in the refrigerator if not used immediately. Makes ¼ cup.

NUTRITIONAL ANALYSIS	
Calories:	39
Total fat:	<1 g
Saturated fat:	<1 g
% calories fat:	12
Carbohydrates:	9 g
Protein:	1 g
Cholesterol:	0 mg
Sodium:	921 mg

Mexico Chili Rub

For poultry, pork or beef.

2 t.	ground cumin
1 t.	ground coriander
3 T.	chili powder
1 T.	brown sugar
1 t.	cinnamon
2 T.	pepper
1 t.	salt

NUTRITIONAL ANALYSIS	
Calories:	39
Total fat:	1 g
Saturated fat:	<1 g
% calories fat:	23
Carbohydrates:	8 g
Protein:	1 g
Cholesterol:	0 mg
Sodium:	635 mg

Mix all ingredients together. Store the rub in a plastic container or bag in the refrigerator if not used immediately. Makes ¼ cup.

Spicy Mustard Rub

Good for poultry.

¼ c.	paprika
2 T.	brown sugar
1 t.	salt
½ t.	pepper
1 t.	dry mustard
1 T.	chili powder

NUTRITIONAL ANALYSIS	
Calories:	42
Total fat:	1 g
Saturated fat:	<1 g
% calories fat:	23
Carbohydrates:	9 g
Protein:	1 g
Cholesterol:	0 mg
Sodium:	535 mg

Mix all ingredients together. Store the rub in a plastic container or bag in the refrigerator if not used immediately. Makes ¼ cup.

Jamaican Rub

For poultry or pork.

¼ c.	sugar
2 T.	onion powder
1 T.	dried thyme
1 t.	nutmeg
½ t.	cloves
2 t.	ground allspice
4 t.	black pepper
2 t.	chili powder
2 t.	salt

NUTRITIONAL ANALYSIS

Calories:	46
Total fat:	<1 g
Saturated fat:	<1 g
% calories fat:	7
Carbohydrates:	11 g
Protein:	<1 g
Cholesterol:	0 mg
Sodium:	609 mg

Mix the ingredients together. Store the rub in a plastic container or bag in the refrigerator up to one week. Makes about ½ cup.

Easy Oriental Rub

For chicken or pork.

3 T.	dry mustard
3 T.	brown sugar
2 T.	five-spice powder

NUTRITIONAL ANALYSIS

Calories:	59
Total fat:	2 g
Saturated fat:	0 g
% calories fat:	33
Carbohydrates:	9 g
Protein:	2 g
Cholesterol:	0 mg
Sodium:	2 mg

Mix the ingredients together. Store the rub in a plastic container or bag in the refrigerator up to one week. Makes about ¼ cup.

The Ultimate Rub

For beef or poultry.

3 T.	brown sugar
$1/4$ t.	ground cumin
1 t.	white pepper
1 t.	black pepper
1 t.	dried thyme
1 t.	ground savory
1 t.	ground coriander
1 t.	dried basil
1 T.	garlic powder
1 T.	onion power
1 T.	dry mustard
2 T.	paprika
dash	salt

NUTRITIONAL ANALYSIS	
Calories:	50
Total fat:	1 g
Saturated fat:	<1 g
% calories fat:	18
Carbohydrates:	10 g
Protein:	1 g
Cholesterol:	0 mg
Sodium:	31 mg

Combine everything in a small bowl and mix well.
Store in the refrigerator up to one month. Makes about ¼ cup.

SAUCES: THE BEST OF THE BEST

These sauce recipes are meant to enhance the wonderful flavor of rotisserie meats, poultry and fish. Serve them on the side, unless otherwise directed, and allow your family and guests to use them according to their own preference. Sauces are typically best when served warm, so use a small dish to retain the heat or reheat, if necessary. There are a few salsa recipes in this section, as well, simply because they go so well with rotisserie fish and poultry on a warm summer evening.

Quick & Easy Barbecue Sauce

For poultry, pork or beef.

½ c.   spicy brown mustard
½ c.   cider vinegar
½ c.   molasses

Mix together and heat in a small saucepan for 3 minutes. Use immediately or refrigerate in a plastic container up to one week. Makes 1½ cups.

NUTRITIONAL ANALYSIS	
Calories:	19
Total fat:	<1 g
Saturated fat:	<1 g
% calories fat:	12
Carbohydrates:	4 g
Protein:	<1 g
Cholesterol:	0 mg
Sodium:	56 mg

Horseradish Sauce

For lamb or beef.

1/4 c.	water
1 T.	olive oil
1 t.	lemon juice
1 t.	pepper
1/2 c.	prepared horseradish

Mix all ingredients and use the sauce to baste the meat while cooking. If not used immediately, refrigerate up to one week. Makes ¾ cup.

NUTRITIONAL ANALYSIS	
Calories:	13
Total fat:	1 g
Saturated fat:	<1 g
% calories fat:	66
Carbohydrates:	1 g
Protein:	<1 g
Cholesterol:	0 mg
Sodium:	27 mg

Lowfat Tartar Sauce

Excellent for fish.

2 c.	fat-free mayonnaise
1/4 c.	fresh lemon juice
2 T.	minced garlic
1 c.	minced red onion
1/2 c.	minced dill pickle
1/2 t.	salt
1/2 t.	pepper

Combine all the ingredients and refrigerate. Store up to one week. Makes 2½ cups sauce.

NUTRITIONAL ANALYSIS	
Calories:	9
Total fat:	0 g
Saturated fat:	0 g
% calories fat:	1
Carbohydrates:	2 g
Protein:	<1 g
Cholesterol:	0 mg
Sodium:	101 mg

Spicy Chili Grilling Sauce

Use with fish or poultry.

1/4 t.	hot pepper sauce
1 T.	minced garlic
1 t.	minced fresh ginger
1 T.	olive oil
2 T.	Worcestershire sauce
1/2 c.	chili sauce
1/4 c.	cider vinegar
1 t.	pepper

NUTRITIONAL ANALYSIS	
Calories:	17
Total fat:	<1 g
Saturated fat:	<1 g
% calories fat:	37
Carbohydrates:	3 g
Protein:	<1 g
Cholesterol:	0 mg
Sodium:	118 mg

Mix all ingredients and serve with fish or poultry.
Refrigerate up to one week in a covered plastic container.
Makes ¾ cup.

Hoisin Barbecue Sauce

For poultry or beef.

2 T.	minced garlic
1 t.	five-spice powder
2 T.	cider vinegar
2 T.	water
$1/2$ c.	tomato sauce
$1/2$ c.	honey
2 T.	hoisin sauce
$1/4$ c.	soy sauce
$1/2$ t.	chili powder

NUTRITIONAL ANALYSIS

Calories: 22
Total fat: <1 g
Saturated fat: 0 g
% calories fat: 2
Carbohydrates: 5 g
Protein: <1 g
Cholesterol: 0 mg
Sodium: 163 mg

Mix all ingredients. Refrigerate up to one week in a covered plastic container. Makes 1½ cups.

Everyday Barbecue Sauce

For beef.

1	6 oz. can tomato paste
1	8 oz. can tomato sauce
2 T.	Worcestershire sauce
1/4 c.	minced onion
3 T.	minced garlic
1 t.	black pepper
1 t.	dry mustard
1 T.	brown sugar
2 T.	cider vinegar
1 T.	chili powder

NUTRITIONAL ANALYSIS	
Calories:	12
Total fat:	<1 g
Saturated fat:	<1 g
% calories fat:	5
Carbohydrates:	3 g
Protein:	<1 g
Cholesterol:	0 mg
Sodium:	58 mg

Mix all ingredients and heat in a small saucepan for 5 minutes. You may either serve this warm with cooked meat or use it as a marinade prior to cooking. Refrigerate up to one week in a covered plastic container. Makes 1½ cups.

Jamaican Barbecue Sauce

For poultry or pork.

3	jalapeño peppers, seeded and finely minced
1 c.	prepared chili sauce
1/4 c.	chopped green onion
3 T.	minced garlic
1 T.	vegetable oil
1 t.	allspice
1 t.	ground ginger
1/2 c.	fat-free chicken broth
1/4 c.	fresh lime juice

NUTRITIONAL ANALYSIS	
Calories:	14
Total fat:	<1 g
Saturated fat:	<1 g
% calories fat:	23
Carbohydrates:	3 g
Protein:	<1 g
Cholesterol:	0 mg
Sodium:	92 mg

Combine all the ingredients and refrigerate. Refrigerate up to one week. Makes 2 cups.

Everyday Salsa

This recipe makes enough to serve today and more for the rest of the week.

¼ c.	chopped red pepper
¼ c.	chopped green pepper
¼ c.	chopped orange pepper
½	minced poblano pepper (more or less, as desired)
1	chopped tomato
½ c.	lime juice
1	6 oz. can tomato juice
1 t.	pepper
½ t.	salt
1 c.	chopped red onion

NUTRITIONAL ANALYSIS

Calories:	4
Total fat:	<1 g
Saturated fat:	0 g
% calories fat:	6
Carbohydrates:	1 g
Protein:	<1 g
Cholesterol:	0 mg
Sodium:	36 mg

Combine all the ingredients and refrigerate to blend the flavors. Makes 2 cups.

Fresh Fruit Salsa

A perfect accompaniment for fish or poultry.

2 c.	chopped ripe peaches
½ c.	chopped ripe papaya
1 T.	chopped red onion
1 T.	fresh lime juice
¼ t.	salt

NUTRITIONAL ANALYSIS

Calories:	6
Total fat:	<1 g
Saturated fat:	0 g
% calories fat:	2
Carbohydrates:	2 g
Protein:	<1 g
Cholesterol:	0 mg
Sodium:	19 mg

Combine the fruit, juice and salt and refrigerate to blend the flavors. Use within 2 days. Makes 2½ cups.

Chapter 3

Appealing Appetizers & Snacks

For those of us who love to eat, appetizers and snacks don't really "count." That is, they may be loaded with high fat and calories, but they aren't *really* part of our daily menu. We don't want to know that those little morsels of food can play a significant role by adding fat to our diets. But, here's the reality about appetizers and snacks: WE LIKE THEM. And, we want to eat and enjoy them without those guilty feelings. That's exactly why this chapter is included in this book. Here you'll find recipes for appetizers and snacks such as Fresh Tomato Bruschetta and HomeBaked Tortilla Chips, but you won't find the high fat that typically goes with them. You can enjoy these appealing appetizers and snacks everyday—they are made for your good health.

A NOTE TO THE COOK

You can reduce the amount of fat in your daily diet by taking some simple steps:

- Keep fresh fruit and vegetables on hand. Whether you have bananas within reach or cut carrots and fresh zucchini in the refrigerator, you are more likely to reach for a healthy alternative if you have fruits and vegetables prepared and ready to eat.

■ Try to think of "non-traditional" snacks instead of the typical chips and crackers. During very hot summer days, my young sons enjoy snack-sized, plastic bags of frozen peas. They like both the flavor and the crunchiness—without realizing they are eating their vegetables.

■ When making dips or spreads, remember that using fat-free or lowfat ingredients for the foundation of the dips is easy. Simply substitute fat-free sour cream, lowfat mayonnaise and reduced-fat cream cheese in dips. Buy lowfat cheeses for spreads. Use nonfat yogurt for your own homemade salad dressing.

■ The powerful flavors of garlic and onion will greatly enhance your appetizer recipes when used in small amounts. Mild flavors from herbs such as parsley won't overpower foods, but they will complement dips and spreads nicely.

■ Use a non-stick cooking spray if you need to fry foods and use a butter-flavored cooking spray for added flavor. Check the labels of these products for a total fat gram count.

1 APPETIZER DIPS & SPREADS

Appetizers are meant to be just that—a bit of food to intrigue your appetite. Serve small portions and try new recipes regularly. Dips and spreads are a great way to introduce new foods and flavors to your family.

Creamy Dill Dip

A perfect partner for Sweet & Tasty Snackin' Carrots (p. 159).

1/2 c.	lowfat cream cheese
4 T.	finely chopped green onion
1/4 c.	buttermilk
2 T.	chopped fresh dill
2 I.	creamy horseradish
1/4 t.	salt
dash	pepper

NUTRITIONAL ANALYSIS

Calories:	33
Total fat:	2 g
Saturated fat:	1 g
% calories fat:	60
Carbohydrates:	2 g
Protein:	2 g
Cholesterol:	7 mg
Sodium:	110 mg

Using a blender or food processor, process the cream cheese until very smooth. Gradually add the green onion, buttermilk, dill, horseradish, salt and pepper. Serves 10. Refrigerate any leftovers.

Cabo Guacamole

This colorful, "good-for-you" dip goes well with HomeBaked Tortilla Chips (p. 48).

1 T.	lemon juice
1	medium ripe avocado
2 T.	chopped cilantro
1/4 c.	lowfat cream cheese
1/2 c.	chopped red onion
2 c.	chopped ripe tomatoes
1/4 t.	tabasco sauce

NUTRITIONAL ANALYSIS	
Calories:	57
Total fat:	4 g
Saturated fat:	1 g
% calories fat:	62
Carbohydrates:	4 g
Protein:	1 g
Cholesterol:	3 mg
Sodium:	24 mg

In a small bowl, combine the lemon juice and avocado. Mix together until smooth. Add the remaining ingredients and serve immediately. Serves 10. Refrigerate any leftovers.

Parmesan Artichoke Spread

This rich, mild-flavored dip goes well with toasted sourdough rounds. Or, for a super-fast entrée, serve this spread over Quick & Easy Rotisserie Chicken Breasts (p. 107).

1	14 oz. can artichoke hearts, well drained
1 T.	finely minced garlic
$1/2$ c.	lowfat mayonnaise
$3/4$ c.	lowfat Parmesan cheese
$1/2$ t.	lemon juice
$1/2$ t.	salt
$1/4$ t.	pepper

NUTRITIONAL ANALYSIS	
Calories:	56
Total fat:	1 g
Saturated fat:	<1 g
% calories fat:	17
Carbohydrates:	4 g
Protein:	7 g
Cholesterol:	6 mg
Sodium:	484 mg

Combine all ingredients in a blender and process until smooth. Pour into a small saucepan and heat until bubbly. Serve immediately. Serves 10. Refrigerate any leftovers.

Pesto Dip

Start a wonderful Italian dinner with this dip and an antipasto tray of carrots, olives, thin-sliced turkey, lowfat mozzarella cheese and fresh tomatoes.

1/2 c.	lowfat mayonnaise
1/2 c.	fat-free sour cream
1/2 c.	lowfat Parmesan cheese
1/2 c.	chopped fresh basil
2 t.	minced garlic
2 oz.	pine nuts

NUTRITIONAL ANALYSIS

Calories:	78
Total fat:	4 g
Saturated fat:	<1 g
% calories fat:	44
Carbohydrates:	4 g
Protein:	8 g
Cholesterol:	5 mg
Sodium:	215 mg

Combine the mayonnaise, sour cream, cheese, basil and garlic. Mix well and refrigerate for 4–6 hours to blend the flavors. Spread the pine nuts on the rotisserie baking sheet. Set the Timer for 6 minutes and bake at 350°F. Sprinkle the pine nuts over the dip just prior to serving. Serves 10. Refrigerate any leftovers.

Pico de Gallo

Everyone's favorite Mexican salsa! Whether you make it mild, hot, or wild, it is versatile enough to be an appetizer, snacking dip or entrée sauce. Try serving it with Herb Roasted Fish Steaks (p. 141).

4 c.	large chopped red tomatoes
1/4 c.	fresh lemon juice
1/2 c.	chopped fresh cilantro
1/2 c.	chopped red onion
2 T.	minced jalapeno pepper (more or less to taste)
2 T.	minced garlic
1/2 t.	salt
1/4 t.	pepper

NUTRITIONAL ANALYSIS	
Calories:	16
Total fat:	<1 g
Saturated fat:	0 g
% calories fat:	10
Carbohydrates:	4 g
Protein:	<1 g
Cholesterol:	0 mg
Sodium:	89 mg

Combine all ingredients in a medium-sized bowl. Cover tightly with plastic wrap and refrigerate 4–12 hours to blend the flavors. Serves 16. Refrigerate any leftovers.

APPETIZERS FOR ALL OCCASIONS

Whether you serve a hot cup of soup to chase the chill from a winter's day or offer a cold vegetable tray to beat the heat, appetizers pave the way for delicious and satisfying meals.

Crostini & Herbed Bean Dip

Just one small slice will awaken your tastebuds!

10	slices crostini, 1/4-inch thick
2 t.	olive oil
1	15 oz. can cooked cannellini beans, drained
1/4 c.	chopped fresh parsley
1/2 t.	chili powder
2 T.	minced garlic
2 T.	fat-free sour cream
1/4 t.	salt
1/4 t.	pepper
1/4 c.	chopped green onion
2 T.	lemon juice
1/4 t.	ground coriander
	fresh parsley

NUTRITIONAL ANALYSIS

Calories:	60
Total fat:	2 g
Saturated fat:	<1 g
% calories fat:	24
Carbohydrates:	9 g
Protein:	2 g
Cholesterol:	<1 mg
Sodium:	180 mg

Place the crostini rounds on the rotisserie baking sheet. Set the Timer for 10 minutes and bake at 400°F. Pause the cooking cycle after 5 minutes and turn the slices. Lightly brush each slice with the olive oil. Resume baking for 5 minutes. Place the crostini on a serving tray. Combine all remaining ingredients in a blender and process until smooth. Top each slice of crostini with a generous mounded tablespoon of bean dip. Garnish each with the parsley. Serves 10. Refrigerate any leftover spread.

Vegetable Antipasto Tray

Serve with Soft Italian Focaccia Breadsticks (p. 187).

15 oz. can garbanzo beans, drained
1 c.   fat-free Italian salad dressing
1/2 c. pitted ripe olives, chilled
1   16 oz. can tiny whole beets, chilled and quartered
1   6 oz. jar hot green chili peppers (optional)
1   6 oz. jar marinated artichoke hearts, well drained
2 c.   chilled celery sticks

NUTRITIONAL ANALYSIS	
Calories:	130
Total fat:	4 g
Saturated fat:	<1 g
% calories fat:	26
Carbohydrates:	22 g
Protein:	3 g
Cholesterol:	0 mg
Sodium:	1170 mg

In a small bowl, pour the Italian salad dressing over the garbanzo beans. Cover tightly and refrigerate 4–6 hours. Drain the beans and place them in a row on an 8" x 10" serving tray. Arrange similar rows with the olives, beets, chili peppers, artichoke hearts and celery. Serves 8.

Marinated Confetti Peppers

Serve these peppers with Teriyaki Rotisserie Chicken (p. 98), to wake up your appetite!

2	red peppers, seeded and cut into $1/2$-inch strips
2	green peppers, seeded and cut into $1/2$-inch strips
2 T.	olive oil
2 T.	minced garlic
1 t.	salt
$1/2$ t.	pepper
$1/2$ t.	dried oregano
1 T.	red wine vinegar

NUTRITIONAL ANALYSIS	
Calories:	39
Total fat:	3 g
Saturated fat:	<1 g
% calories fat:	75
Carbohydrates:	2 g
Protein:	<1 g
Cholesterol:	0 mg
Sodium:	292 mg

Place pepper strips in a shallow glass pan. Combine remaining ingredients in a small bowl and pour over the peppers, turning to coat evenly. Cover the pan tightly with plastic wrap and marinate in the refrigerator 6–12 hours. Drain and serve. Serves 8.

Fresh Tomato Bruschetta

This popular appetizer is also a healthy introduction to any meal.

2	large ripe red tomatoes, chopped
1/2 c.	chopped red onion
2 T.	finely minced fresh parsley
2 T.	finely minced fresh basil
1 t.	balsamic vinegar
1 t.	olive oil
2 T.	minced garlic
1	French or sourdough baguette
2 t.	olive oil
2 T.	lowfat grated Parmesan cheese

NUTRITIONAL ANALYSIS

Calories: 69
Total fat: 2 g
Saturated fat: <1 g
% calories fat: 6
Carbohydrates: 48 g
Protein: 7 g
Cholesterol: 1 mg
Sodium: 227 mg

Combine tomatoes, onion, parsley, basil, vinegar, oil and garlic in a medium bowl. Cut the bread into 20 slices and place on the rotisserie baking sheet. Set the Timer for 10 minutes and bake at 400°F. Pause the cooking cycle after 5 minutes and turn the slices. Brush the slices lightly with olive oil and resume baking for 5 minutes. Cool slightly. Mound a heaping spoonful of the tomato mixture on each slice of bread. Sprinkle Parmesan cheese over each slice. Serve warm or cold.
Serves 10, 2 slices per person.

HomeBaked Tortilla Chips

These very lowfat chips take the place of the typical high-fat commercial chips. They are especially good when served warm.

12	8-inch corn tortillas
1/2 t.	garlic powder
1 t.	seasoned salt
	butter-flavored cooking spray

NUTRITIONAL ANALYSIS	
Calories:	58
Total fat:	<1 g
Saturated fat:	0 g
% calories fat:	10
Carbohydrates:	12 g
Protein:	1 g
Cholesterol:	0 mg
Sodium:	158 mg

Place 4 tortillas on the rotisserie baking sheet. Coat each tortilla lightly with cooking spray. Sprinkle tortillas with garlic powder and seasoned salt and cut each tortilla into 8 wedges. Set the Timer for 15 minutes and bake at 425°F. Remove the chips and cool. Continue baking the remaining tortillas. Store in a sealed plastic bag. Serves 12, 8 chips per person.

Spicy New Mexico Soup

This lovely soup warms up a winter day.

1	skinless, boneless chicken breast half
2	slices turkey bacon, cut into small pieces
1 c.	chopped onion
1 t.	olive oil
1	14 oz. can fat-free chicken broth
2	16 oz. cans whole kernel corn, drained
2 c.	water
1	4 oz. can chopped green chiles, drained
2 T.	minced garlic
1 t.	pepper
1/2 t.	salt
1/4 c.	fat-free sour cream

NUTRITIONAL ANALYSIS	
Calories:	247
Total fat:	4 g
Saturated fat:	<1 g
% calories fat:	15
Carbohydrates:	38 g
Protein:	18 g
Cholesterol:	31 mg
Sodium:	745 mg

Place the chicken in the adjustable basket of the rotisserie as directed in the Owner's Manual. Set the Timer for 15 minutes and cook at 425°F. Cool and shred into small pieces. Lightly sauté the bacon and onion in the olive oil in a large soup pot. Add the shredded chicken, broth, corn, water, green chiles, garlic, pepper and salt. Simmer 30 minutes. Just before serving, add the sour cream and stir until smooth and heated through. Serves 6.

3 SNACKS

These snacks are not only tasty—they are healthy additions to your daily eating plan. Remember that although these snacks are low in fat, they still contain calories, so enjoy each snack in moderation.

Delicious Deviled Eggs

These eggs have all the traditional flavor you love—without the fat. Try serving these with Summer Vegetable Kebabs (p. 156), for a light luncheon.

6	hard-cooked eggs
1 1/4 c.	fat-free liquid egg product
1/2 c.	lowfat mayonnaise
1/2 t.	horseradish
1/2 t.	Dijon mustard
1/2 t.	vinegar
1/4 t.	salt
1/4 t.	pepper
	paprika

NUTRITIONAL ANALYSIS

Calories: 71
Total fat: 3 g
Saturated fat: <1 g
% calories fat: 44
Carbohydrates: <1 g
Protein: 9 g
Cholesterol: 106 mg
Sodium: 225 mg

Cut the hard-cooked eggs in half and discard the yolks. Chill the egg white halves for 10 minutes. Lightly coat a small sauté pan with vegetable spray and scramble the egg product until cooked through. Cool for 5 minutes. Combine scrambled eggs, mayonnaise, horseradish, mustard, vinegar, salt and pepper in a blender or food processor and process until very smooth. Scoop the egg mixture into egg white halves and sprinkle the tops of each with a bit of paprika. Refrigerate until serving and refrigerate any leftovers. Serves 12.

Sausage & Cheese Mini Snack Pizzas

A favorite teen snack.

6	English muffins, split
1 c.	prepared pizza sauce
3	turkey sausage links, cooked and sliced into $1/4$-inch pieces
$1/4$ c.	chopped onion
$1/4$ c.	fresh sliced mushrooms
$1/2$ c.	shredded lowfat mozzarella cheese

NUTRITIONAL ANALYSIS

Calories:	193
Total fat:	3 g
Saturated fat:	<1 g
% calories fat:	14
Carbohydrates:	31 g
Protein:	11 g
Cholesterol:	13 mg
Sodium:	608 mg

Place the muffin halves on the rotisserie baking sheet. Cover each with the prepared pizza sauce. Top with sausage slices, onion and mushrooms. Sprinkle mozzarella cheese over each muffin. Slide the baking sheet into the rotisserie, as directed in the Owner's Manual. Set the Timer for 15 minutes and bake at 450°F. Carefully remove pizzas from the oven. Serves 6, 2 pizzas per person.

Mexicali Tostadas

Everyone's favorite!

6	corn tortillas
1 T.	olive oil
1/4 t.	garlic salt
1	16 oz. can fat-free refried beans
1/2 c.	fat-free sour cream
1	small chopped onion
1 c.	fat-free Monterey jack cheese
1	large chopped tomato
3 c.	chopped lettuce

NUTRITIONAL ANALYSIS

Calories: 210
Total fat: 3 g
Saturated fat: <1 g
% calories fat: 13
Carbohydrates: 32 g
Protein: 14 g
Cholesterol: 5 mg
Sodium: 593 mg

Place tortillas on the rotisserie baking sheet. Brush the tortillas with olive oil and sprinkle with garlic salt. Set the Timer for 15 minutes and bake at 425°F. Place tortillas on 6 individual plates. In a small saucepan, warm the refried beans until heated through. Top each tortilla with a generous layer of refried beans. Cover beans with sour cream and top with onion, cheese, tomatoes and lettuce. Serves 6.

AirBaked Onion Potatoes

The yummy flavor of fresh, warm potatoes without the heavy fat!

8   potatoes, washed and sliced into $1/2$-inch strips
1 t.   onion powder
$1/4$ t.   paprika

Place the potatoes into the roasted veggie/air bake basket of the rotisserie as directed by the Owner's Manual. Set the Timer for 45 minutes and cook at 425°F. Pause the cooking cycle and season the potatoes with the onion powder and paprika. Turn the basket to coat the potatoes evenly. Resume cooking for an additional 15 minutes. Serves 8.

NUTRITIONAL ANALYSIS	
Calories:	119
Total fat:	<1 g
Saturated fat:	<1 g
% calories fat:	1
Carbohydrates:	28 g
Protein:	3 g
Cholesterol:	0 mg
Sodium:	6 mg

Fresh Vegetable Kebabs

A handy way to take advantage of summer's fresh vegetable bounty.

2	medium fresh zucchini, cut in $1/2$-inch slices
10	ripe cherry tomatoes
1	medium green pepper, cut into chunks
1	medium red pepper, cut into chunks
1	small red onion, cut into chunks
1	fresh lemon, cut in half
$1/4$ t.	pepper

NUTRITIONAL ANALYSIS

Calories:	48
Total fat:	<1 g
Saturated fat:	<1 g
% calories fat:	8
Carbohydrates:	10 g
Protein:	3 g
Cholesterol:	0 mg
Sodium:	7 mg

Thread the fresh vegetables on the skewers, alternating each. Drizzle the lemon juice over each skewer and sprinkle with pepper. Place the skewers into the rotisserie as directed by the Owner's Manual. Set the timer for 20 minutes and cook at 425°F. Vegetables should be slightly firm and warm when ready to serve. Serves 4.

Vegetable Stuffed Mushrooms

Heat and serve as snacks or a light luncheon entrée.

¹/₂ c.	packaged herb seasoned stuffing mix, crumbled
¹/₄ c.	lowfat margarine, melted
¹/₄ c.	finely chopped carrot
¹/₄ c.	finely chopped green pepper
2 T.	minced onion
1 T.	chopped fresh parsley
¹/₂ t.	Italian seasoning
¹/₂ t.	salt
¹/₄ t.	pepper
16	2-inch fresh mushrooms, stems removed

NUTRITIONAL ANALYSIS

Calories:	77
Total fat:	3 g
Saturated fat:	<1 g
% calories fat:	37
Carbohydrates:	10 g
Protein:	2 g
Cholesterol:	0 mg
Sodium:	352 mg

Combine the stuffing mix, margarine, carrots, green peppers, onions, parsley and seasonings in a small bowl. Place the mushrooms on the rotisserie baking sheet. Top each with one heaping spoonful of the vegetable mixture. Place the mushrooms in the rotisserie as directed by the Owner's Manual. Set the Timer for 12 minutes and cook at 425°F. Remove and serve immediately. Serves 8, 2 mushrooms per person.

Sweet Cherries with Orange Dip

A refreshing combination! Serve as a snack or an appetizer for a light dinner entrée, such as Basil & Citrus Turkey Breast (p. 101).

2 c.	fat-free sour cream
2 T.	packed brown sugar
1 T.	orange juice
1 T.	grated orange peel
3 c.	fresh cherries, rinsed

NUTRITIONAL ANALYSIS	
Calories:	155
Total fat:	<1 g
Saturated fat:	<1 g
% calories fat:	3
Carbohydrates:	31 g
Protein:	6 g
Cholesterol:	7 mg
Sodium:	69 mg

In a small bowl combine sour cream, sugar, orange juice and peel. Chill for 2–4 hours to blend the flavors. Serve the fruit dip with the sweet cherries. Serves 6. Refrigerate any leftovers.

Chapter 4

Delicious Rotisserie Meats

The rotisserie process seals in so much flavor while the fat drips away that few spices are needed to create truly flavorful roasts, chops, steaks and kebabs. However, because we all enjoy a variety of tastes, this chapter offers a selection of recipes that will inspire cooks every day of the week. From Grandma's Peppered Beef Roast and Hawaiian Pork Roast to Teriyaki Flank Steak and Mint & Rosemary Lamb Kebabs, you'll find recipes that eliminate much of the fat while offering you the best flavors.

A NOTE TO THE COOK

You can eliminate some of the fat of traditional meat recipes by following the suggestions listed below:

- When cooking a roast, eliminate the fatty gravy that typically goes with it. If you like, substitute a fat-free au jus broth or make a lowfat glaze instead.

- Trim all visible fat from the meat before cooking.

- Look for cuts of meat that naturally have less fat, such as rump roasts and flank steaks. If you are unsure of which cuts of meat have less fat, ask the butcher to help you make some selections.

The amount of "marbling," which is the visible fat disbursed throughout the meat, will determine the fat content of your cut, so look at each selection carefully.

- Use herbs and spices to create new tastes for meat choices, rather than relying on high-fat sauces. Rotisserie meats are very tender and delicious with just a touch of spicing. In fact, the wonderful natural flavor of the meat will surface if the meats are *not* overly spiced and sauced.

- Keep your portions small. According to the U.S. Department of Agriculture, an adequate serving of beef is 3 ounces per person.

ROTISSERIE MEAT TEMPERATURES

Use this quick guide to determine the correct temperature for cooked meat. To test the meat accurately, use a meat thermometer.

BEEF

Rare	140°F
Medium	160°F
Well Done	170°F

PORK

Well Done	160°F

LAMB

Medium	145°F
Well Done	160°F

1 BEEF ROASTS, STEAKS & MORE

There is nothing quite like the aroma of beef on a rotisserie, slowly roasting on a Sunday afternoon. Add the fragrance of garlic and pepper along with it, and you have all the elements that will bring your family to the table in a flash. Whether you choose to rotisserie a roast, steak or kebabs, you can enjoy these beef recipes, knowing that they are easy to prepare and healthful, too.

Grandma's Peppered Beef Roast

A classic!

1	4 lb. beef rump roast
1 t.	salt
2 t.	pepper
1 t.	garlic salt

NUTRITIONAL ANALYSIS	
Calories:	318
Total fat:	15 g
Saturated fat:	6 g
% calories fat:	45
Carbohydrates:	<1 g
Protein:	42 g
Cholesterol:	124 mg
Sodium:	442 mg

Remove any visible fat from the roast and tie with cooking string. Center the rump roast on the rotisserie bar. Generously rub the spices over the roast to coat evenly. Place the roast in the rotisserie as directed by the Owner's Manual. Set the Timer for 1½–2 hours and cook at 350°F. Allow the beef to rest 10 minutes after cooking. Thinly slice across the grain. Serves 12.

Vegetable Stuffed Roast

The stuffing inside keeps the beef very moist and gives it a delectable flavor.

1	4 lb. boneless beef sirloin roast
1 c.	finely chopped onion
1/2 c.	finely chopped celery
1/2 c.	finely chopped green pepper
1 t.	olive oil
1 t.	salt
2 t.	pepper
1 t.	minced garlic
1/2 t.	dry mustard
1/2 t.	chili powder
	salt and pepper

NUTRITIONAL ANALYSIS

Calories:	201
Total fat:	6 g
Saturated fat:	2 g
% calories fat:	29
Carbohydrates:	2 g
Protein:	32 g
Cholesterol:	91 mg
Sodium:	294 mg

Make 5 deep slits in the roast, forming pockets that extend down to 1/2-inch from the bottom of the roast. Do not cut all the way through the roast. In a small bowl, mix the onion, celery, green pepper, oil, salt, pepper, garlic, mustard and chili powder. Scoop a heaping tablespoon of the vegetable mixture and place into each pocket. Use cooking string to tie the roast at 2 to 3-inch intervals. (It's better to use more string than less rather than risk losing the stuffing while the roast cooks). Carefully center the roast on the rotisserie bar and prepare it for the rotisserie according to the Owner's Manual. Set the Timer for 1½–2 hours and cook at 350°F. After cooking, let the roast rest for 10 minutes. Slice carefully. Serves 12.

Rich Beef Roast

A very light, fragrant basting sauce makes this roast memorable.

1	5 lb. beef sirloin roast
1 t.	salt
1 t.	pepper
1½ c.	lowfat beef broth
2 T.	lowfat margarine
2 T.	chopped parsley

NUTRITIONAL ANALYSIS	
Calories:	198
Total fat:	7 g
Saturated fat:	2 g
% calories fat:	32
Carbohydrates:	<1 g
Protein:	32 g
Cholesterol:	91 mg
Sodium:	275 mg

Tie the roast with cooking string and sprinkle it with the salt and pepper. Prepare the roast for the rotisserie as directed by the Owner's Manual. Set the Timer for 2–2½ hours and cook at 350°F. While the beef is cooking, make the sauce by heating the broth, margarine and parsley until warm. Do not boil. Pause the cooking cycle every 30 minutes and baste the roast with the sauce. When the cooking cycle is done, remove the beef from the rotisserie and let it rest for 10 minutes. Slice thinly. Serves 15.

Tandoori Rotisserie Beef

The marinade gives this roast an exotic taste.

1	4 lb. beef cross rib roast
2 T.	tomato paste
1 t.	paprika
2 t.	chili powder
1 T.	lemon juice
1 t.	curry powder
1 T.	minced garlic
1 c.	nonfat plain yogurt
1 c.	finely chopped onion

NUTRITIONAL ANALYSIS

Calories:	208
Total fat:	6 g
Saturated fat:	2 g
% calories fat:	26
Carbohydrates:	4 g
Protein:	33 g
Cholesterol:	91 mg
Sodium:	112 mg

Tie the roast with cooking string and place it in a shallow glass pan. Combine all remaining ingredients to make a thick sauce. Pour over the roast, turning the roast to coat evenly. Cover the roast tightly with plastic wrap and refrigerate 8–12 hours to blend the flavors. Turn the roast occasionally. Remove the roast from the marinade and discard any unused marinade. Prepare the roast for the rotisserie as directed in the Owner's Manual. Set the Timer for 1½–2 hours and cook at 350°F. Allow the beef to rest 10 minutes after cooking. Slice thinly and serve. Serves 12.

Pepper Crusted Roast

Spicy, but good!

1		4 lb. rolled beef rump roast
1 t.		olive oil
1 T.		minced fresh garlic
1 T.		fresh cracked pepper

Tie the rump roast with cooking string. Center the roast on the rotisserie bar. Mix together the oil, garlic and pepper and generously rub over the roast. Place the roast in the rotisserie as directed by the Owner's Manual. Set the Timer for 1½–2 hours and cook at 350°F. Allow the beef to rest 10 minutes after cooking. Slice thinly and serve. Serves 12.

NUTRITIONAL ANALYSIS	
Calories:	322
Total fat:	16 g
Saturated fat:	6 g
% calories fat:	46
Carbohydrates:	<1 g
Protein:	42 g
Cholesterol:	124 mg
Sodium:	97 mg

Red Hot Barbecue Beef

Perfect for a summer evening. Serve with Crunchy Cucumber Salad (p. 171), to put out the fire!

1/2 t.	cumin
1 T.	chili powder
1 t.	olive oil
2 t.	lemon juice
2 T.	balsamic vinegar
1 t.	brown sugar
1 T.	chopped fresh oregano
1 T.	minced garlic
1/4 c.	tomato sauce
1	1 lb. beef flank steak

NUTRITIONAL ANALYSIS	
Calories:	193
Total fat:	11 g
Saturated fat:	4 g
% calories fat:	50
Carbohydrates:	3 g
Protein:	20 g
Cholesterol:	51 mg
Sodium:	138 mg

In a small bowl, combine cumin, chili powder, oil, lemon juice, vinegar, brown sugar, oregano, garlic and tomato sauce. Mix thoroughly. Place the steak in a shallow glass pan and pour the marinade over it, turning to coat evenly. Cover the steak with plastic wrap and refrigerate 4–12 hours. Place the steak in the adjustable basket as directed in the Owner's Manual and discard any remaining marinade. Set the Timer for 20–25 minutes and cook at 450°F. Let the steak rest for 5 minutes and slice thinly across the grain. Serves 6.

Teriyaki Flank Steak

This family favorite has become so well-known by friends over the years that many of them now request it when invited to our home for dinner!

1	1 lb. beef flank steak
1/4 c.	soy sauce
2 T.	vegetable oil
2 T.	water
1/4 c.	chopped green onion
1 T.	ground ginger
2 T.	cider vinegar
2 T.	honey
2 T.	minced garlic

NUTRITIONAL ANALYSIS

Calories:	246
Total fat:	14 g
Saturated fat:	5 g
% calories fat:	52
Carbohydrates:	9 g
Protein:	21 g
Cholesterol:	51 mg
Sodium:	749 mg

Place the steak in a shallow glass pan. Combine all remaining ingredients and pour the marinade over the steak, turning to coat evenly. Cover the steak with plastic wrap and refrigerate 4–12 hours. Place the steak in the adjustable basket as directed in the Owner's Manual and discard any remaining marinade. Set the Timer for 20–25 minutes and cook at 450°F. Let the steak rest for 5 minutes and slice thinly across the grain. Serves 6.

Northern Italy Stuffed Steak

The mushrooms and olives add juicy, subtle flavor to these small sirloin steaks.

4	4 oz. beef sirloin steaks
1 T.	olive oil
1 T.	chopped chives
½ t.	basil
2 c.	thinly sliced mushrooms
2 c.	thinly sliced black olives

NUTRITIONAL ANALYSIS	
Calories:	263
Total fat:	16 g
Saturated fat:	3 g
% calories fat:	53
Carbohydrates:	7 g
Protein:	24 g
Cholesterol:	62 mg
Sodium:	650 mg

Mix together the oil, chives, basil, mushrooms and olives. Slit each steak along one side to form a deep pocket (resembling pita bread). Slice to within ½-inch of the bottom of the steak, but do not slice all the way through. Fill each pocket with one-fourth of the mushroom and olive mixture and tie the steaks with cooking string to hold in place. Place the steaks in the adjustable basket as directed in the Owner's Manual. Set the Timer for 20–25 minutes and cook at 450°F. Serves 4.

Dijon Mustard Steaks

The Dijon gives these small dinner steaks a distinctive flavor.

4	4 oz. beef sirloin steaks
1/2 c.	Dijon mustard
1 T.	olive oil
1 T.	minced garlic
1 t.	dried oregano
1 t.	dried thyme
1/2 t.	dried basil

NUTRITIONAL ANALYSIS	
Calories:	207
Total fat:	11 g
Saturated fat:	3 g
% calories fat:	48
Carbohydrates:	4 g
Protein:	23 g
Cholesterol:	62 mg
Sodium:	804 mg

Place the steaks in a shallow glass pan. Combine the mustard, oil, garlic and spices to make a thick sauce. Brush each steak with the mustard mixture and turn to coat both sides. Cover the steaks with plastic wrap and marinate in the refrigerator for 2–4 hours to blend the flavors. Place the steaks in the adjustable basket as directed in the Owner's Manual. Discard any remaining sauce. Set the Timer for 20–25 minutes and cook at 450°F. Serves 4.

Garlic Pesto Kebabs

These beef and vegetable kebabs have a delicious Italian flavor.

³/₄ c.	chopped fresh basil
2 T.	minced garlic
1 t.	oregano
1 t.	lemon pepper
1 t.	salt
2 T.	olive oil
1	1 lb. beef top sirloin steak, cut into 1-inch pieces
1	medium onion, cut into chunks
16	2-inch fresh mushrooms, cleaned and stems removed

NUTRITIONAL ANALYSIS

Calories:	189
Total fat:	10 g
Saturated fat:	2 g
% calories fat:	46
Carbohydrates:	7 g
Protein:	19 g
Cholesterol:	50 mg
Sodium:	584 mg

Combine basil, garlic, oregano, lemon pepper, salt and oil in a blender and process until smooth. Thread the skewers with pieces of steak, onions and mushrooms, alternating each on the skewers. Brush each skewer with the pesto mixture. Place the skewers on the wire rack as directed in the Owner's Manual. Set the Timer for 25–30 minutes and cook at 450°F. Pause the cooking cycle after 10 minutes and brush the kebabs with additional pesto. Resume cooking. Serves 5.

Cozumel Beef Fajitas

Everyone can join in to assemble these outstanding fajitas.

1	1 lb. beef flank steak
3 T.	olive oil
1/4 c.	lime juice
1 t.	Worcestershire sauce
1/2 t.	sugar
2 t.	red chile pepper flakes
2 T.	minced garlic
1	onion, thinly sliced

Accompaniments:
warm flour tortillas
fat-free sour cream
fresh salsa
sliced green onions
sliced black olives

NUTRITIONAL ANALYSIS

Calories:	246
Total fat:	16 g
Saturated fat:	5 g
% calories fat:	60
Carbohydrates:	4 g
Protein:	20 g
Cholesterol:	51 mg
Sodium:	72 mg

Place the steak in a shallow glass pan. Combine oil, juice, Worcestershire sauce, sugar, red pepper flakes, garlic and onion in a small bowl. Mix well and pour over the steak. Refrigerate 12 hours to blend the flavors. Place the steak in the adjustable basket as directed in the Owner's Manual and discard any remaining marinade. Set the Timer for 20–25 minutes and cook at 450ºF. Let the steak rest for 5 minutes and slice thinly across the grain. Place the steak into warm flour tortillas and add your choice of accompaniments. Serves 6.

Oriental Steak Kebabs

Serve these kebabs with mixed vegetables and steamed rice for a well-balanced meal.

1	1 lb. beef sirloin steak, cut into 1-inch cubes
1/4 c.	soy sauce
1/4 c.	cider vinegar
2 T.	minced garlic
1/4 t.	ground allspice
1/4 t.	ground ginger
1/4 c.	chopped green onion
1/4 c.	water
1 T.	honey

NUTRITIONAL ANALYSIS	
Calories:	158
Total fat:	5 g
Saturated fat:	2 g
% calories fat:	28
Carbohydrates:	6 g
Protein:	21 g
Cholesterol:	60 mg
Sodium:	869 mg

Place the steak cubes into a shallow glass pan. Combine all the remaining ingredients and pour over the steak, turning to coat evenly. Refrigerate 12–24 hours. Thread the steak cubes onto the skewers and place in the rotisserie as directed in the Owner's Manual. Discard any remaining marinade. Set the Timer for 25–30 minutes and cook at 450°F. Serves 5.

Warm Steak Salad

A small amount of steak goes a long way in this unusual recipe.

1	$1/2$ lb. beef top sirloin steak
2 c.	torn leafy green lettuce
2 c.	torn iceberg lettuce
2 c.	torn red leaf lettuce
1	10 oz. can mandarin oranges, well-drained

Dressing:

2 T.	rice wine vinegar
1 T.	minced garlic
$1/2$ t.	chili powder
1 T.	sesame oil
2 t.	Worcestershire sauce
1 t.	sugar
$1/4$ t.	salt
$1/4$ t.	pepper

NUTRITIONAL ANALYSIS	
Calories:	194
Total fat:	6 g
Saturated fat:	2 g
% calories fat:	30
Carbohydrates:	12 g
Protein:	19 g
Cholesterol:	50 mg
Sodium:	221 mg

Remove any visible fat from the steak. Place the steak in the adjustable basket of the rotisserie as directed by the Owner's Manual. Set the Timer for 20 minutes and cook at 450°F until medium-well done. While the steak is cooking, mix all the dressing ingredients and shake well to combine flavors. Thinly slice the steak. In a large serving dish, combine steak, mandarin oranges and mixed greens. Pour the dressing over the salad and toss well. Serve immediately. Garnish with chopped green onion, if desired. Serves 4.

Hearty Beef Stroganoff

This new version has all the flavor with much less fat.

1	1 lb. beef top round
2 t.	pepper
1 t.	vegetable oil
1 c.	chopped onion
1	10 oz. can 99% fat-free cream of mushroom soup
2 c.	thinly sliced mushrooms
1 t.	pepper
8 oz.	wide egg noodles
1 c.	fat-free sour cream

NUTRITIONAL ANALYSIS	
Calories:	343
Total fat:	6 g
Saturated fat:	3 g
% calories fat:	17
Carbohydrates:	37 g
Protein:	26 g
Cholesterol:	80 mg
Sodium:	250 mg

Remove all visible fat from the meat. Coat the meat generously with the pepper and place the beef in the adjustable basket as directed by the Owner's Manual. Set the Timer for 15 minutes and cook at 450°F. The beef should be rare when you remove it from the rotisserie. On a clean cutting board, cut the beef into very thin slices and set aside. Heat the oil in a large sauté pan and cook the onions for 2 minutes. Add the cream of mushroom soup, mushrooms and the pepper and heat through. Simmer gently.
In a large pot, bring 3 quarts of water to a boil. Add the noodles and stir. Cook noodles approximately 7 minutes or until tender. Drain and keep the noodles warm. Add the beef slices and the sour cream to the mushroom sauce and mix gently to combine flavors. Add more pepper, if desired. Spoon the sauce over the cooked noodles. Serves 6.

Herbed Veal Rotisserie Roast

Veal is naturally low in fat and this mild marinade complements it very well.

1	3 lb. boneless shoulder veal roast
2 T.	olive oil
2 T.	water
1 T.	cider vinegar
1 T.	sugar
1 t.	chopped fresh basil
2 T.	chopped fresh parsley
1 t.	chopped fresh thyme
1 t.	salt
$1/_2$ t.	pepper
1 T.	minced garlic

NUTRITIONAL ANALYSIS	
Calories:	149
Total fat:	7 g
Saturated fat:	2 g
% calories fat:	43
Carbohydrates:	2 g
Protein:	19 g
Cholesterol:	79 mg
Sodium:	299 mg

Tie the veal with cooking string and place it in a shallow glass pan. Combine the remaining ingredients and mix well. Pour the marinade over the veal, turning to coat evenly. Cover tightly with plastic wrap and refrigerate 4–12 hours. Prepare the roast for the rotisserie as directed by the Owner's Manual. Set the Timer for 1½–2 hours and cook at 350°F. Allow the veal to rest 10 minutes after cooking. Slice thinly. Serves 8–10.

PORK ROASTS, CHOPS & MORE

If you enjoy mild-flavored meat, with a healthy amount of protein and surprisingly low amounts of fat, try the pork recipes in this chapter. You'll not only discover how good pork can really taste, you will also find out how very versatile pork can be. Don't be surprised when your family and guests ask for more!

Herbed Pork Roast

Marinate this roast overnight to develop the wonderful mustard and herb flavors.

1	3 lb. boneless pork loin roast
3 T.	Dijon mustard
1 c.	minced onion
3 T.	minced garlic
2 T.	paprika
2 t.	black pepper
2 t.	dried thyme
1 t.	celery seed
1 t.	ground sage
2 t.	chili powder

NUTRITIONAL ANALYSIS

Calories:	305
Total fat:	12 g
Saturated fat:	4 g
% calories fat:	36
Carbohydrates:	7 g
Protein:	41 g
Cholesterol:	117 mg
Sodium:	198 mg

Tie the roast with cooking string and place it in a medium glass bowl. Rub the surface of the roast with the Dijon mustard. Combine the onion, garlic, paprika, pepper, thyme, celery seed, sage and chili powder in a small bowl. Mix well and sprinkle generously over the roast, turning the roast to coat evenly. Cover the roast with plastic wrap and refrigerate 8–12 hours. Prepare the roast for the rotisserie as directed in the Owner's Manual. Set the Timer for 1½–2 hours and cook at 350°F. The roast is done when the internal temperature is 160°F on the meat thermometer. Let the meat rest for 15 minutes and slice thinly to serve. Serves 8–10.

Southern Party Pork Roast

A sweet and tangy marinade gives this roast just the right touch.

1	5 lb. boneless pork loin roast
2 T.	dry mustard
1/2 c.	Worcestershire sauce
1/2 c.	hot sauce (as preferred)
2 t.	salt
2 T.	minced garlic
2 T.	chopped fresh parsley
1 c.	chopped onion
2 T.	steak sauce
1	8 oz. can tomato sauce
3 T.	brown sugar
1 t.	yellow mustard

NUTRITIONAL ANALYSIS	
Calories:	335
Total fat:	13 g
Saturated fat:	7 g
% calories fat:	36
Carbohydrates:	7 g
Protein:	45 g
Cholesterol:	130 mg
Sodium:	595 mg

Place the roast in a shallow glass pan. In a small bowl, combine the remaining ingredients and mix well. With a sharp knife, make several deep slits in the roast and fill each with the herb sauce. Rub the remaining sauce over the roast, coating evenly. Tie the roast with cooking string. Cover the roast with plastic wrap and refrigerate for 12 hours. Prepare the roast for the rotisserie as directed in the Owner's Manual. Discard any unused sauce. Set the Timer for 2–2½ hours and cook at 350°F. The roast is done when the internal temperature is 160°F on the meat thermometer. Let the meat rest for 15 minutes and slice thinly to serve. Serves 15.

Rotisserie Baked Ham for a Crowd

This is a very easy and delicious way to feed hungry guests!

1	5 lb. lowfat, fully-cooked, boneless ham
1 c.	packed brown sugar
½ t.	dry mustard
1 T.	cider vinegar

NUTRITIONAL ANALYSIS	
Calories:	219
Total fat:	5 g
Saturated fat:	2 g
% calories fat:	21
Carbohydrates:	19 g
Protein:	25 g
Cholesterol:	65 mg
Sodium:	1263 mg

Tie the ham with cooking string and place it on the rotisserie bar, as directed in the Owner's Manual. Combine the sugar with the mustard and vinegar and brush over the entire ham, coating evenly. Set the Timer for 1½ hours and cook at 350°F. After cooking, allow the ham to rest for 5 minutes and slice thinly. Serves 15.

Hawaiian Pork Roast

Serve with fresh papaya for a "change of pace" dinner.

1	3 lb. boneless pork loin roast
1 T.	lime juice
1 T.	minced garlic
1 T.	Dijon mustard
1 T.	brown sugar
2 T.	soy sauce
1/4 t.	ground ginger
1/4 c.	honey
1/4 c.	unsweetened pineapple juice

NUTRITIONAL ANALYSIS

Calories:	307
Total fat:	11 g
Saturated fat:	4 g
% calories fat:	34
Carbohydrates:	9 g
Protein:	40 g
Cholesterol:	117 mg
Sodium:	321 mg

Tie the roast with cooking string and place it in a shallow glass pan. Combine all the remaining ingredients and mix well. Pour the marinade over the roast, turning it to coat evenly. Refrigerate for 4–12 hours, turning occasionally. Prepare the roast for the rotisserie as directed in the Owner's Manual. Discard any unused marinade. Set the Timer for 1½–2 hours and cook at 350°F. The roast is done when the internal temperature is 160°F on the meat thermometer. Let the meat rest for 15 minutes and slice thinly to serve. Serves 8–10.

Spicy Country Pork Ribs

Robust spices and a zesty sauce make these ribs really special!

³/₄ c.	cider vinegar
¹/₂ t.	chili pepper
¹/₂ t.	black pepper
3 lbs.	lean, country-style pork ribs
¹/₄ c.	salsa
¹/₄ c.	brown sugar
¹/₄ c.	water
¹/₄ c.	Worcestershire sauce
2 t.	chili powder

NUTRITIONAL ANALYSIS	
Calories:	233
Total fat:	12 g
Saturated fat:	5 g
% calories fat:	49
Carbohydrates:	6 g
Protein:	24 g
Cholesterol:	78 mg
Sodium:	126 mg

Mix together the vinegar, chili powder and black pepper. Cut the ribs into individual pieces, remove any visible fat and place in a shallow glass pan. Pour the vinegar and spices over the ribs, turning to coat evenly. Refrigerate for 2–4 hours, basting occasionally. Place the ribs in the adjustable basket as directed in the Owner's Manual. Set the Timer for 2–2¹/₂ hours and cook at 350°F. Pause the cooking cycle after 1 hour and baste the ribs with the vinegar sauce again. Resume cooking. While the ribs are cooking, combine the salsa, brown sugar, water, Worcestershire sauce and chili powder in a small saucepan and simmer for 3–4 minutes or until slightly thickened. The ribs are fully cooked when the temperature is 160°F on the meat thermometer. Serve the ribs with the sauce on the side. Serves 4.

Sunday Night Pork Roast

Easy to make, tempting to eat!

1	3 lb. boneless pork loin roast
1/4 c.	brown spicy mustard
3 T.	soy sauce
1/2 t.	tabasco sauce

NUTRITIONAL ANALYSIS	
Calories:	278
Total fat:	12 g
Saturated fat:	4 g
% calories fat:	39
Carbohydrates:	<1 g
Protein:	40 g
Cholesterol:	117 mg
Sodium:	465 mg

Tie the roast with cooking string and place it in a shallow glass pan. Combine the mustard, soy sauce and tabasco sauce and rub over the roast, turning to coat evenly. Cover the roast with plastic wrap and refrigerate for 1 hour. Prepare the roast for the rotisserie as directed in the Owner's Manual. Set the Timer for 1½–2 hours and cook at 350°F. The roast is done when the internal temperature is 160°F on the meat thermometer. Let the meat rest for 15 minutes and slice thinly to serve. Serves 8–10.

Saucy Ham Slices

A sweet and tangy glaze covers these slices while they cook. Fast and easy!

1	fully cooked, boneless, lowfat smoked ham slice, 1-inch thick
1/4 c.	packed brown sugar
2 T.	prepared horseradish
2 T.	fresh lemon juice

NUTRITIONAL ANALYSIS

Calories:	69
Total fat:	<1 g
Saturated fat:	<1 g
% calories fat:	9
Carbohydrates:	15 g
Protein:	2 g
Cholesterol:	3 mg
Sodium:	205 mg

Score each side of the ham slice with a sharp knife, about 1/4-inch deep. Combine the sugar, horseradish and juice in a small saucepan and heat to boiling, stirring to dissolve sugar. Brush the ham slice on both sides with the glaze mixture. Place the ham in the adjustable basket, as directed by the Owner's Manual. Set the Timer for 15 minutes and cook at 450°F. Pause the cooking cycle after 8 minutes and brush the glaze over the ham slice again. Do not touch the hot heating elements. Resume the cooking cycle. Discard any remaining glaze. Serves 4.

Barbecued Pork Tenderloin

A tangy mustard sauce wakes up the tenderloin.

- ¼ c. spicy brown mustard
- ¼ c. cider vinegar
- ¼ c. molasses
- 1 lb. pork tenderloin, ¾-inch thick

Combine the mustard, vinegar and molasses in a small bowl and blend thoroughly. Brush the barbecue sauce over both sides of each piece of tenderloin. Place the pork in the adjustable basket as directed in the Owner's Manual.
Set the Timer for 20–25 minutes and cook at 425°F.
Serves 4.

NUTRITIONAL ANALYSIS	
Calories:	209
Total fat:	5 g
Saturated fat:	2 g
% calories fat:	22
Carbohydrates:	16 g
Protein:	25 g
Cholesterol:	67 mg
Sodium:	251 mg

Rotisserie Ham & Sweet Potato Bake

Add a green salad and dinner is complete!

¹/₂ c.	packed brown sugar	
¹/₄ c.	prepared horseradish	
2 T.	lemon juice	
4	sweet potatoes	
1	I lb. fully cooked, lowfat, boneless ham slice	

NUTRITIONAL ANALYSIS	
Calories:	221
Total fat:	1 g
Saturated fat:	<1 g
% calories fat:	5
Carbohydrates:	51 g
Protein:	4 g
Cholesterol:	3 mg
Sodium:	495 mg

Combine the sugar, horseradish and lemon juice in a small bowl and blend thoroughly. Cut the sweet potatoes in ¹/₂-inch cubes and place in the roasted veggie/air bake basket, as directed in the Owner's Manual. Set the Timer for 40 minutes and cook at 425°F. Place the cooked potatoes on an ovenproof serving plate and keep warm in a 200°F oven. Place the ham steak in the adjustable basket and brush with one-half of the sauce. Set the Timer for 15 minutes and cook at 450°F. Drizzle the remaining sauce over the sweet potatoes. Divide the ham and sweet pototoes evenly on four individual plates. Serves 4.

Spicy Pork Tenderloin

A fast entrée that will delight everyone in the family.

1 T.	chili powder
1/4 t.	dried oregano
1/4 t.	salt
1/4 t.	Italian seasoning
1/4 t.	ground cumin
1 T.	minced garlic
1	1 lb. pork tenderloin

NUTRITIONAL ANALYSIS

Calories:	148
Total fat:	4 g
Saturated fat:	1 g
% calories fat:	28
Carbohydrates:	2 g
Protein:	24 g
Cholesterol:	67 mg
Sodium:	215 mg

Combine chili powder, oregano, salt, Italian seasoning, cumin and garlic in a small bowl. Generously press the spice mixture into the pork, coating each side. Place the tenderloin in the adjustable basket as directed in the Owner's Manual. Set the Timer for 20–25 minutes and cook at 425°F. Slice the tenderloin thinly and serve. Serves 4.

Italian Tomato Pork Chops

A hearty tomato and pepper sauce coats these tender chops.

4	pork loin chops, 3/4-inch thick
1 t.	minced garlic
1 t.	olive oil
1	14 oz. can stewed tomatoes
1 t.	dried oregano
1/2 t.	salt
1/2 t.	pepper
1/4 c.	water
2 T.	cornstarch
1	onion, thinly sliced
1	green pepper, thinly sliced

NUTRITIONAL ANALYSIS

Calories:	146
Total fat:	4 g
Saturated fat:	1 g
% calories fat:	28
Carbohydrates:	15 g
Protein:	11 g
Cholesterol:	28 mg
Sodium:	515 mg

Remove all visible fat from the chops. Place the chops into the adjustable basket of the rotisserie, as directed by the Owner's Manual. Set the Timer for 20–25 minutes and cook at 425°F. While chops are cooking, prepare the sauce. In a medium saucepan, heat the garlic in the oil. Add the tomatoes, dried oregano, salt, and pepper. In a small bowl, mix the water and cornstarch together and add to the tomato sauce. Heat and stir until thickened. Just before serving, mix in the onion and pepper. Add additional salt and pepper, if desired. Arrange the cooked chops on a large serving platter and cover with the sauce. Serves 4.

Spicy Pork & Vegetable Kebabs

A quick and easy complete dinner.

1 T.	minced garlic
¹/₄ c.	chopped green onion
2 T.	chili powder
1 T.	chopped fresh parsley
¹/₄ c.	fat-free chicken broth
3 T.	lime juice
1	1 lb. pork tenderloin, cut into 1-inch chunks
1	red pepper, cut into 1-inch chunks
2	ears of corn, cut into 2-inch chunks
2	potatoes, cut into 2-inch chunks

NUTRITIONAL ANALYSIS	
Calories:	264
Total fat:	5 g
Saturated fat:	2 g
% calories fat:	17
Carbohydrates:	29 g
Protein:	27 g
Cholesterol:	65 mg
Sodium:	106 mg

In a small bowl combine the garlic, green onion, chili powder, parsley, chicken broth and juice. Place the cubed tenderloin pieces in a shallow glass pan and cover with one-half of the marinade. Refrigerate for 1 hour. When ready to rotisserie, thread the pork cubes onto 2 skewers and discard the unused marinade. Thread the peppers, corn and potatoes on 3 skewers, alternating vegetables. Coat the vegetables with the remaining one-half of the marinade. Place the skewers in the rotisserie as directed in the Owner's Manual. Set the Timer for 25–30 minutes and cook at 450°F. After 15 minutes, pause the cooking cycle and brush the vegetables and pork with the marinade. Resume the cooking cycle. When the pork and vegetables are ready, divide the meat and vegetables evenly onto 4 plates. Serves 4.

LAMB ROASTS, CHOPS & MORE

Lamb has a rich, smooth flavor and partners especially well with garlic and other spices that develop the full potential of this tender meat. Look for fresh lamb in the supermarket and remember to trim all visible fat from the meat.

Herbed Lamb Kebabs with Summer Vegetables

Serve with crusty French bread and fruit for a complete meal.

		NUTRITIONAL ANALYSIS	
2 T.	olive oil	Calories:	199
1/2 c.	fresh lemon juice	Total fat:	13 g
1 t.	salt	Saturated fat:	3 g
1/2 t.	pepper	% calories fat:	54
1 T.	dried rosemary	Carbohydrates:	11 g
2 T	minced garlic	Protein:	13 g
1	1 lb. boneless lamb, cut into 1-inch cubes	Cholesterol:	33 mg
12	2-inch mushrooms	Sodium:	622 mg
2	small zucchini, cut into 1-inch slices		
12	cherry tomatoes		

Combine the oil, lemon juice, salt, pepper, rosemary and garlic in a small bowl. Thread the lamb, mushrooms, zucchini and tomatoes onto skewers, as directed in the Owner's Manual and brush well with the marinade. Set the Timer for 25–30 minutes and cook at 400°F.

Classic Boneless Lamb Roast

A tangy orange sauce accompanies this lovely roast.

1	3 lb. boneless leg of lamb roast
1/4 t.	pepper
2 T.	cider vinegar
2 T.	honey
1 c.	orange marmalade
1 T.	minced garlic
3/4 c.	spicy brown mustard

NUTRITIONAL ANALYSIS	
Calories:	296
Total fat:	9 g
Saturated fat:	3 g
% calories fat:	26
Carbohydrates:	26 g
Protein:	29 g
Cholesterol:	87 mg
Sodium:	320 mg

Combine pepper, vinegar, honey, marmalade, garlic and mustard in a small bowl. Tie the roast with cooking string, place it in a shallow glass pan and pour the marinade over it. Cover the roast with plastic wrap and refrigerate for 4–12 hours. Prepare the roast for the rotisserie as directed in the Owner's Manual. Set the Timer for 1½–2 hours and cook at 350°F. The roast is done when the internal temperature is 145°F on the meat thermometer. Let the meat rest for 15 minutes and slice thinly to serve. Serves 8–10.

Mint & Rosemary Lamb Kebabs

The fresh mint and herbs accentuate the richness of these lamb kebabs.

1	1 lb. boneless lamb shoulder, cut into 1-inch cubes
1/2 c.	chopped onion
1 T.	minced garlic
1/4 c.	cider vinegar
2 T.	olive oil
1/4 c.	water
1 T.	honey
1 T.	dried rosemary
1 T.	chopped fresh mint
1/2 t.	salt
1/2 t.	pepper
1	medium onion, cut into chunks
6	plum tomatoes, cut in half
12	small fresh mushrooms

NUTRITIONAL ANALYSIS

Calories:	317
Total fat:	17 g
Saturated fat:	4 g
% calories fat:	46
Carbohydrates:	18 g
Protein:	26 g
Cholesterol:	79 mg
Sodium:	376 mg

Place lamb cubes in a shallow glass pan. Combine the chopped onion, garlic, vinegar, oil, water, honey, rosemary, mint, salt and pepper in a small bowl and mix thoroughly. Pour the marinade over the lamb and cover tightly with plastic wrap. Refrigerate for 4–12 hours, turning meat occasionally. When ready to rotisserie, thread the lamb cubes on 2 skewers. Discard the remaining marinade. Thread the onion, tomatoes and mushrooms on 3 skewers, alternating vegetables on each. Place the skewers in the rotisserie as directed in the Owner's Manual. Set the Timer for 25–30 minutes and cook at 400°F. When the lamb and vegetables are ready, divide onto four warmed plates. Serves 4.

Chapter 5

Tender Rotisserie Poultry

Without a doubt, poultry can be one of the most healthy and delicious additions to your daily diet. According to leading sources of nutritional information, skinless turkey and chicken breast lead the way in lowfat protein. Because your rotisserie cooks poultry by sealing in flavorful juices and eliminating the fat, the rotisserie method of cooking is additionally healthy for everyone. And, if that isn't good enough news, here's more—the flavor and versatility of poultry can satisfy even the most demanding appetites. Take a look at some of the recipes that follow in this chapter and let your tastebuds take over! From Tandoori Chicken and Lemon Cornish Game Hens to Mediterranean Chicken & Vegetable Kebabs and Barbecued Chicken Pizza, you'll find in this chapter a wealth of flavors to enjoy.

A NOTE TO THE COOK

Be very careful when handling fresh poultry. Although any raw meat needs to be handled properly, raw poultry carries bacteria that can be especially harmful to people. Here are some ways to prevent contamination:

■ Wrap and freeze poultry immediately after purchasing, unless you plan to use it within 2 days (in that case, refrigerate it). To freeze correctly, wrap a layer of aluminum foil or plastic around the poultry container and put it into a plastic freezer bag. Remove as much air as possible.

■ Always defrost poultry in the refrigerator, never at room temperature. Again, that bacteria thrives in warm temperatures! Keep poultry very, very cold until cooking.

■ After handling poultry, clean all utensils, cutting boards, and towels with hot water and antibacterial soap. Do NOT cross-contaminate foods or cooking surfaces.

■ Mother always knew best! Wash your hands with antibacterial soap and warm water before handling poultry—and wash them again after you've handled poultry.

■ Never serve poultry that is less than well cooked (approximately 170–180°F). When well cooked, poultry juices run clear and the meat is white with no pink color inside. For best results, use a meat thermometer to test poultry before you begin to carve.

■ If the poultry is not fully cooked after the designated cooking time, reset the rotisserie timer for an additional 5–10 minutes and resume the cooking cycle. Test again for best results.

■ Marinades can easily become contaminated with bacteria, either through the utensils used or because of exposure to raw meats. Because of this, you will probably want to discard the marinade rather than using it as a sauce on the cooked meat. If you do want to use the marinade as a sauce, boil it for at least five minutes to remove any contamination.

1 NICE & EASY POULTRY: ROTISSERIE "WHOLE BIRD" ROASTING

If the thought of roasting a whole bird makes you nervous, just try it once. You'll discover, as millions of rotisserie lovers have, that it's an easy way to create stunning and delectable meals. You don't have to become involved in complicated recipes or time-consuming preparations to rotisserie a whole bird successfully. Simply marinate your poultry with herbs or dust it with a few spices and sit back to let the rotisserie do the work for you. The only thing you have to prepare for are all the compliments you'll receive!

Sunday's Best Rotisserie Chicken

Here's the easiest rotisserie recipe you'll find and it's probably one of the best! Try roasting one large chicken or two smaller chickens so you'll have prepared, cooked chicken ready for another day of the week.

1	5–6 lb. whole roasting chicken
1 t.	seasoned salt
1 t.	garlic powder
	salt & pepper to cover chicken

Remove the giblets from the chicken and discard. Wash the cavity well and dry with paper towels. Tie the chicken wings and legs with cooking string Evenly rub the spices onto the chicken skin to coat well. Prepare the chicken for the rotisserie as directed in the Owner's Manual. Set the Timer and cook for 1½–2 hours at 350°F. The chicken is fully cooked when the juices run clear and the meat is white, with no pink remaining. If the chicken is not fully cooked, reset the Timer for an additional 10 minutes and test again. If desired, use a meat thermometer to test the internal temperature (175–180°F). Serves 4.

NUTRITIONAL ANALYSIS

With skin

Calories: 538

Total fat: 32 g

Saturated fat: 9 g

% calories fat: 55

Carbohydrates: <1 g

Protein: 58 g

Cholesterol: 182 mg

Sodium: 559 mg

Without skin

Calories: 288

Total fat: 7 g

Saturated fat: 2 g

% calories fat: 21

Carbohydrates: 5 g

Protein: 50 g

Cholesterol: 155 mg

Sodium: 777 mg

Fabulous "Fast Food" Rotisserie Chicken

This chicken tastes unbelievably like the expensive fast-food chicken!

1	5–6 lb. whole roasting chicken
2 T.	vegetable oil
1 T.	honey
2 T.	lemon juice
1/4 t.	paprika
dash	seasoned salt

Remove the giblets from the chicken and discard. Wash the cavity well and dry with paper towels. Combine oil, honey, lemon juice, paprika and seasoned salt in a saucepan and simmer 2 minutes. Tie the chicken wings and legs with cooking string. Prepare the chicken for the rotisserie as directed in the Owner's Manual. With a soft pastry brush, lightly cover the chicken completely with the honey glaze. Set the Timer for 1½–2 hours and cook at 350°F. After 30 minutes of cooking, pause the rotisserie and lightly baste again. Resume the rotisserie cooking cycle. The chicken is fully cooked when the juices run clear and the meat is white, with no pink remaining. If the chicken is not fully cooked, reset the Timer for an additional 10 minutes and test again. If desired, use a meat thermometer to test the internal temperature (175–180°F). Discard any remaining marinade. Serves 4.

NUTRITIONAL ANALYSIS

With skin
Calories: 614
Total fat: 39 g
Saturated fat: 10 g
% calories fat: 58
Carbohydrates: 5 g
Protein: 58 g
Cholesterol: 182 mg
Sodium: 197 mg

Without skin
Calories: 343
Total fat: 13 g
Saturated fat: 3 g
% calories fat: 36
Carbohydrates: 5 g
Protein: 48 g
Cholesterol: 155 mg
Sodium: 200 mg

Deli Rotisserie Chicken

This recipe is straight from the grocery deli, where that wonderful aroma of rotisserie chicken always makes shoppers immediately hungry.

1	5–6 lb. whole roasting chicken
1 t.	salt
2 t.	paprika
1 t.	chili powder
1 t.	garlic powder
2 t.	black pepper
1 t.	onion powder
1 t.	dried thyme

NUTRITIONAL ANALYSIS

With skin
Calories: 549
Total fat: 32 g
Saturated fat: 9 g
% calories fat: 54
Carbohydrates: 3 g
Protein: 58 g
Cholesterol: 155 mg
Sodium: 768 mg

Without skin
Calories: 278
Total fat: 7 g
Saturated fat: 2 g
% calories fat: 23
Carbohydrates: 3 g
Protein: 49 g
Cholesterol: 155 mg
Sodium: 768 mg

Remove the giblets from the chicken and discard. Wash the cavity well and dry with paper towels. Tie the chicken wings and legs with cooking string. Combine all the spices in a small bowl and mix well. Rub thoroughly into the skin of the chicken, pressing gently. Cover the chicken and refrigerate overnight. Prepare the chicken for the rotisserie as directed in the Owner's Manual. Set the Timer for 1½–2 hours and cook at 350°F. The chicken is fully cooked when the juices run clear and the meat is white, with no pink remaining. If the chicken is not fully cooked, reset the Timer for an additional 10 minutes and test again. If desired, use a meat thermometer to test the internal temperature (175–180°F). Serves 4.

Oktoberfest Rotisserie Chicken

The basting sauce for this flavorful chicken also browns the chicken beautifully.

1	5–6 lb. roasting chicken, whole
2 T.	paprika
1 t.	salt
1 t.	black pepper
$\frac{1}{2}$ c.	nonfat milk
$\frac{1}{4}$ c.	lemon juice
$\frac{1}{4}$ c.	lime juice

Remove the giblets from the chicken and discard. Wash the cavity well and dry with paper towels. Combine paprika, salt, pepper, milk, and juices. Tie the chicken wings and legs with cooking string. Place the chicken in the rotisserie as directed in the Owner's Manual. Brush the chicken completely with the basting sauce. Set the Timer for 1½–2 hours and cook at 350°F. After 30 minutes, pause the rotisserie and lightly baste again. Do not touch the heating elements. Resume the rotisserie cooking cycle. Discard any remaining sauce. The chicken is fully cooked when the juices run clear and the meat is white, with no pink remaining. If the chicken is not fully cooked, reset the Timer for an additional 10 minutes and test again. If desired, use a meat thermometer to test the internal temperature (175–180°F). Serves 4.

NUTRITIONAL ANALYSIS

With skin
Calories: 559
Total fat: 32 g
Saturated fat: 9 g
% calories fat: 54
Carbohydrates: 5 g
Protein: 59 g
Cholesterol: 183 mg
Sodium: 773 mg

Without skin
Calories: 289
Total fat: 7 g
Saturated fat: 2 g
% calories fat: 21
Carbohydrates: 5 g
Protein: 50 g
Cholesterol: 155 mg
Sodium: 777 mg

Spicy Asian Barbecued Chicken

Hoisin is a rich, thick oriental sauce. It can be found in the oriental section of your supermarket.

1	3–4 lb. whole roasting chicken
1/4 c.	hoisin sauce
1/4 c.	chili sauce
2 t.	dry mustard
2 T.	olive oil
1/4 t.	chili powder
1/4 c.	orange juice

Remove the giblets from the chicken and discard. Wash the cavity well and dry with paper towels. Tie the chicken wings and legs with cooking string. Combine hoisin sauce, chili sauce, mustard, oil, chili powder and orange juice. Place the chicken in a large bowl or plastic container and cover with marinade. Turn to coat evenly. Securely wrap and marinate 4–6 hours in the refrigerator. Place the chicken on the rotisserie bar, following the Owner's Manual instructions. Set the Timer and cook for 1¼–1½ hours at 350°F. Discard remaining marinade. The chicken is fully cooked when the juices run clear and the meat is white, with no pink remaining. If the chicken is not fully cooked, reset the Timer for an additional 10 minutes and test again. If desired, use a meat thermometer to test the internal temperature (175–180°F). Serves 2–3.

NUTRITIONAL ANALYSIS

With skin
Calories: 885
Total fat: 53 g
Saturated fat: 13 g
% calories fat: 55
Carbohydrates: 18 g
Protein: 79 g
Cholesterol: 244 mg
Sodium: 885 mg

Without skin
Calories: 524
Total fat: 19 g
Saturated fat: 3 g
% calories fat: 34
Carbohydrates: 18 g
Protein: 67 g
Cholesterol: 207 mg
Sodium: 889 mg

Sicilian Herb Rotisserie Chicken

Savory Italian chicken at it's best!

1	5–6 lb. whole roasting chicken
1 t.	chopped fresh sage
1 t.	chopped fresh parsley
1/2 t.	chopped fresh thyme
1 t.	chopped fresh rosemary
2 T.	minced garlic

Remove the giblets from the chicken and discard. Wash the cavity well and dry with paper towels. Tie the chicken wings and legs with cooking string. Combine the herbs and garlic thoroughly to make a rub. Generously press into the chicken skin as evenly as possible. Place the chicken in a glass pan and cover with plastic wrap. Refrigerate for 4–6 hours. Prepare the chicken for the rotisserie as directed in the Owner's Manual. Set the Timer for 1½–2 hours and cook at 350°F. The chicken is fully cooked when the juices run clear and the meat is white, with no pink remaining. If the chicken is not fully cooked, reset the Timer for an additional 10 minutes and test again. If desired, use a meat thermometer to test the internal temperature (175–180°F). Serves 4.

NUTRITIONAL ANALYSIS

With skin
Calories: 539
Total fat: 32 g
Saturated fat: 9 g
% calories fat: 55
Carbohydrates: <1 g
Protein: 58 g
Cholesterol: 182 mg
Sodium: 176 mg

Without skin
Calories: 269
Total fat: 7 g
Saturated fat: 2 g
% calories fat: 23
Carbohydrates: <1 g
Protein: 49 g
Cholesterol: 155 mg
Sodium: 179 mg

Teriyaki Rotisserie Chicken

The sweet and sour ingredients in this recipe combine to make a delicious taste sensation.

1	3–4 lb. whole roasting chicken
1/4 c.	soy sauce
1/2 c.	olive oil
1/2 c.	sliced green onion
1 T.	ground ginger
2 T.	honey
2 T.	minced garlic
2 T.	cider vinegar

NUTRITIONAL ANALYSIS

With skin
Calories: 691
Total fat: 40 g
Saturated fat: 13 g
% calories fat: 56
Carbohydrates: 18 g
Protein: 53 g
Cholesterol: 162 mg
Sodium: 1532 mg

Without skin
Calories: 558
Total fat: 33 g
Saturated fat: 5 g
% calories fat: 55
Carbohydrates: 13 g
Protein: 50 g
Cholesterol: 153 mg
Sodium: 987 mg

Remove the giblets from the chicken and discard. Wash the cavity well and dry with paper towels. Mix all marinade ingredients together and stir thoroughly. Tie the chicken wings and legs with cooking string and place in a glass pan. Cover with the marinade, turning to coat evenly. Wrap the chicken tightly in plastic wrap and refrigerate 4–6 hours. Prepare the chicken for the rotisserie as directed in the Owner's Manual. Discard any remaining marinade. Set the Timer for 1¼–1½ hours and cook at 350°F. The chicken is fully cooked when the juices run clear and the meat is white, with no pink remaining. If the chicken is not fully cooked, reset the Timer for an additional 10 minutes and test again. If desired, use a meat thermometer to test the internal temperature (175–180°F). Serves 2–3.

Basil & Garlic Rotisserie Chicken

Subtle flavors create a lovely entrée.

1	3–4 lb. whole roasting chicken
1/4 c.	nonfat chicken broth
2 T.	cider vinegar
2 T.	olive oil
2 T.	minced garlic
1 T.	chopped fresh parsley
1 T.	chopped fresh basil
1/2 t.	salt
1/2 t.	pepper

NUTRITIONAL ANALYSIS

With skin

Calories: 445
Total fat: 31 g
Saturated fat: 7 g
% calories fat: 63
Carbohydrates: 2 g
Protein: 39 g
Cholesterol: 121 mg
Sodium: 520 mg

Without skin

Calories: 265
Total fat: 13 g
Saturated fat: 2 g
% calories fat: 46
Carbohydrates: 2 g
Protein: 33 g
Cholesterol: 103 mg
Sodium: 523 mg

Remove the giblets from the chicken and discard. Wash the cavity well and dry with paper towels. Tie the chicken legs and wings with cooking string. In a small bowl, combine the broth, vinegar, oil, garlic, parsley, basil, salt and pepper. Place the chicken in a shallow glass pan and pour the marinade over it, turning the chicken to cover thoroughly. Marinate in the refrigerator for 4–6 hours. Prepare the chicken for the rotisserie as directed in the Owner's Manual. Discard any remaining marinade. Set the Timer and cook 1 1/4–1 1/2 hours at 350°F. The chicken is fully cooked when the juices run clear and the meat is white, with no pink remaining. If the chicken is not fully cooked, reset the Timer for an additional 10 minutes and test again. If desired, use a meat thermometer to test the internal temperature (175–180°F). Serves 2–3.

Classic Rotisserie Turkey

Enough to feed the entire family and a few more, this savory turkey will delight everyone!

1	16 lb. whole turkey, thawed
1 T.	salt
1 T.	pepper
1 T.	dry mustard
1 T.	chili powder
¼ c.	paprika
¼ c.	brown sugar

NUTRITIONAL ANALYSIS

Calories:	277
Total fat:	13 g
Saturated fat:	4 g
% calories fat:	43
Carbohydrates:	2 g
Protein:	37 g
Cholesterol:	105 mg
Sodium:	309 mg

Remove the giblets from the turkey and discard. Wash the cavity well and dry with paper towels. Combine salt, pepper, dry mustard, chili powder, paprika and brown sugar in a small bowl. Tie the turkey legs and wings with cooking string. Rub the spice mixture thoroughly into the skin of the turkey, pressing gently. Using the 4-prong Meat Tines, attach the turkey to the Rotisserie Bar. Center it carefully to ensure even roasting. Prepare the turkey for the rotisserie as directed in the Owner's Manual. Set the Timer for 4½ hours and cook at 350°F. When cooking time is complete, check the temperature of the turkey by inserting a meat thermometer into the thickest part of the thigh. Do not allow the tip of the thermometer to touch bone. When fully cooked, the internal temperature of the turkey should read 175–180°F. If the turkey is not done, reset the Timer for an additional 15–20 minutes at 350°F and test again. The juices should run clear and there should be no pink meat visible. Allow the turkey to rest for 5–10 minutes before carving. To store any leftover meat, remove from the bone, wrap in airtight aluminum foil or plastic wrap and place in a freezer bag. Frozen turkey should be used within 1 month. Serves 32 people.

Basil & Citrus Turkey Breast

A tangy marinade dresses up this healthful entrée.

1	3–3 ½ lb. boneless turkey breast
1 c.	nonfat chicken broth
2 T.	cider vinegar
½ c.	orange juice
½ t.	black pepper
2 T.	minced fresh basil

NUTRITIONAL ANALYSIS

Calories:	266
Total fat:	10 g
Saturated fat:	3 g
% calories fat:	36
Carbohydrates:	2 g
Protein:	40 g
Cholesterol:	101 mg
Sodium:	103 mg

Place the turkey breast in a deep glass dish. Mix the marinade ingredients and pour over the turkey breast, turning to coat evenly. Cover tightly with plastic wrap. Marinate 4–6 hours in the refrigerator, turning occasionally. Prepare the turkey for the rotisserie as directed in the Owner's Manual. Discard any remaining marinade. Set the Timer for 1½ hour and cook at 350°F. The turkey is fully cooked when the juices run clear and the meat is white, with no pink remaining. If the turkey is not fully cooked, reset the Timer for an additional 10 minutes and test again. If desired, use a meat thermometer to test the internal temperature (175–180°F). Cool slightly and slice thinly. Serves 10.

Pesto Rotisserie Turkey Breast

The bold accent of pesto combines with the rich flavor of turkey.

1	4–5 lb. boneless turkey breast
¹/₂ c.	olive oil
1 c.	nonfat chicken broth
¹/₂ c.	chopped fresh cilantro
¹/₄ c.	lime juice
¹/₄ c.	minced garlic
2 c.	prepared pesto sauce
¹/₂ c.	toasted pine nuts

NUTRITIONAL ANALYSIS

Calories:	419
Total fat:	17 g
Saturated fat:	4 g
% calories fat:	38
Carbohydrates:	3 g
Protein:	60 g
Cholesterol:	158 mg
Sodium:	282 mg

Place the turkey breast in a deep glass dish. Mix oil, broth, cilantro, lime juice and minced garlic in a small bowl. Pour over the turkey breast, turning to coat evenly. Cover tightly with plastic wrap. Marinate 4–6 hours in the refrigerator, turning occasionally. Prepare the turkey for the rotisserie as directed in the Owner's Manual. Discard any remaining marinade. Set the Timer for 1½–2 hours and cook at 350°F. The turkey is fully cooked when the juices run clear and the meat is white, with no pink remaining. If the turkey is not fully cooked, reset the Timer for an additional 10 minutes and test again. If desired, use a meat thermometer to test the internal temperature (175–180°F). Cool for 10 minutes. Slice breast meat thinly and serve with the pesto sauce and toasted pine nuts. Serves 10.

Lemon Cornish Game Hens

Just right for a romantic dinner for two!

2	1¹/₂ lb. Cornish game hens
	butter-flavored cooking spray
¹/₂ t.	black pepper
1 t.	salt
2 t.	chopped fresh parsley
¹/₂ c.	fresh lemon juice
1 T.	balsamic vinegar
2 T.	water

NUTRITIONAL ANALYSIS

With skin

Calories:	690
Total fat:	47 g
Saturated fat:	13 g
% calories fat:	62
Carbohydrates:	7 g
Protein:	58 g
Cholesterol:	367 mg
Sodium:	1331 mg

Without skin

Calories:	317
Total fat:	9 g
Saturated fat:	2 g
% calories fat:	25
Carbohydrates:	7 g
Protein:	52 g
Cholesterol:	233 mg
Sodium:	1305 mg

Remove the giblets from the game hens and discard. Wash each cavity well and dry with paper towels. Tie the hen legs and wings with cooking string. Coat the game hens lightly with the butter-flavored cooking spray. Combine the pepper, salt and parsley and rub well onto hens. Prepare the hens for the rotisserie as directed in the Owner's Manual. Set the Timer for 30 minutes and cook at 400°F. In a small bowl combine the lemon juice, vinegar and water. Pause the cooking cycle after 15 minutes and brush the game hens with the lemon juice glaze. Discard glaze mixture and resume the cooking cycle. The game hens are fully cooked when the juices run clear and the meat is white, with no pink remaining. If desired, use a meat thermometer to test the internal temperature (175–185°F). If the game hens are not fully cooked, reset the Timer for an additional 5–10 minutes and test again. Serves 2.

Duck à l'Orange

A classic French preparation for this rich, full-flavored poultry.

1	4–5 lb. whole duck
1 T.	lowfat margarine
3 T.	finely minced onion
1/4 t.	dried tarragon leaves
1/2 c.	orange juice
1/4 t.	salt
1/4 t.	dry mustard
1/4 c.	raspberry jelly
2 T.	finely shredded orange peel
2 T.	cider vinegar
1	medium orange, peeled and cut into small cubes
2 t.	cornstarch

NUTRITIONAL ANALYSIS

Calories:	164
Total fat:	7 g
Saturated fat:	3 g
% calories fat:	37
Carbohydrates:	12 g
Protein:	13 g
Cholesterol:	48 mg
Sodium:	122 mg

Remove the giblets from the duck and discard. Wash the cavity well and dry with paper towels. In a small saucepan, melt lowfat margarine and sauté the onion until tender. Stir in tarragon. Add the orange juice, salt, mustard, raspberry jelly, and orange peel. Stir and simmer 2 minutes to melt the jelly. Add the vinegar and orange cubes to the sauce and stir gently. Set aside one half of the marinade to use as the sauce. Tie the duckling legs and wings with cooking string. Prepare the duckling for the rotisserie as directed in the Owner's Manual. With a soft pastry brush, lightly cover the duckling completely with the marinade. Set the Timer for 1¾ hours and cook at 400°F. After 1 hour, pause the rotisserie and lightly baste again. (Discard any remaining marinade. Do not combine this marinade with the other half of the unused marinade). Do not touch the heating elements. Resume the rotisserie cooking cycle. The duck is fully cooked when the juices run clear and the meat is white, with no pink remaining. If the duck is not fully cooked, reset the Timer for an additional 10 minutes and test again. If desired, use meat thermometer to test internal temperature (175–180°F). In a small saucepan, stir the cornstarch into the remaining one-half of the marinade. Heat and stir until the sauce thickens and is smooth. Pour the glaze over the duckling just before serving. Serves 8.

Garlic Roasted Cornish Game Hens

Spicy flavors accompany this mild poultry.

2	1¹/₂ lb. Cornish game hens
1 T.	minced garlic
2 t.	salt
1 t.	black pepper
3 T.	lime juice
¹/₄ c.	finely chopped fresh cilantro
¹/₄ c.	finely chopped fresh parsley

Remove the giblets from the game hens and discard. Wash each cavity well and dry with paper towels. Tie the legs and wings with cooking string. Combine garlic, salt, pepper, lime juice, cilantro and parsley in a small bowl. Place the game hens in a shallow glass pan and cover with the marinade, turning to coat evenly. Cover and refrigerate for 4–6 hours. Prepare the game hens for the rotisserie as directed in the Owner's Manual. Discard any remaining marinade. Set the Timer for 30 minutes and cook at 425°F. The hens are fully cooked when the juices run clear and the meat is white, with no pink remaining. If the hens are not fully cooked, reset the Timer for an additional 5 minutes and test again. If desired, use a meat thermometer to test the internal temperature (175–180°F). Serves 2.

NUTRITIONAL ANALYSIS

With skin

Calories:	684
Total fat:	47 g
Saturated fat:	13 g
% calories fat:	62
Carbohydrates:	4 g
Protein:	58 g
Cholesterol:	337 mg
Sodium:	2498 mg

Without skin

Calories:	310
Total fat:	9 g
Saturated fat:	2 g
% calories fat:	26
Carbohydrates:	4 g
Protein:	52 g
Cholesterol:	233 mg
Sodium:	2742 mg

2 DELICIOUS & LOWFAT POULTRY: RECIPES FOR EASY, EVERYDAY MEALS

Whether you are cooking for two or a crowd, poultry naturally lends itself to delicious meals. And, because these dishes are lowfat and healthful for you, you and your family can enjoy them often. Choose from "traditional" favorite recipes offered here, or some of the recipes that come from faraway places. In any event, you'll find "good-for-you" recipes to satisfy all appetites.

Quick & Easy Rotisserie Chicken Breasts

Many favorite recipes call for cooked chicken and using the adjustable basket of your rotisserie to cook the chicken makes it easy! One boneless, skinless chicken breast half typically equals about 1-1½ cups of cooked chicken.

2   boneless, skinless chicken breast halves

NUTRITIONAL ANALYSIS	
Calories:	189
Total fat:	4 g
Saturated fat:	1 g
% calories fat:	21
Carbohydrates:	0 g
Protein:	36 g
Cholesterol:	97 mg
Sodium:	85 mg

Trim any visible fat from the chicken. Place the chicken breasts in the adjustable basket of the rotisserie as directed in the Owner's Manual. Set the Timer for 15 minutes and cook at 425°F. Remove the chicken breasts and cool slightly. Shred, chop or dice as desired. Refrigerate for up to 3 days. Makes 2–3 cups cooked chicken.

Italian Rotisserie Chicken Breasts

The marinade in this recipe adds a sophisticated taste to the mild chicken flavor.

4	boneless, skinless chicken breast halves
1/2 c.	fat-free Italian salad dressing
1/4 c.	fat-free chicken broth
1 T.	olive oil
1 T.	lemon juice
1 t.	grated lemon peel
1/2 t.	dried Italian seasoning
2 T.	chopped green onion
1/4 t.	black pepper

NUTRITIONAL ANALYSIS

Calories: 207
Total fat: 6 g
Saturated fat: 1 g
% calories fat: 29
Carbohydrates: 8 g
Protein: 27 g
Cholesterol: 73 mg
Sodium: 441 mg

Place the chicken breasts in a shallow glass pan. Combine the dressing, broth, oil, juice, lemon peel, seasoning, onions and pepper in a small bowl. Pour over the chicken breasts and seal the dish tightly with plastic wrap. Marinate for 4–12 hours, turning occasionally. Place the chicken in the adjustable basket of the rotisserie, following the Owner's Manual directions. Set the Timer for 15 minutes and cook at 425°F. The chicken is done when the juices run clear and there is no pink color visible. Discard any remaining marinade. Serves 4.

Sweet & Sour Chicken

Serve over hot steamed rice for an outstanding "any-night-of-the-week" meal.

4	boneless, skinless chicken breast halves
1/4 c.	lemon juice
1/4 t.	black pepper
1 T.	olive oil
2 T.	cider vinegar
2 T.	brown sugar, packed
1/4 c.	ketchup
1/2 c.	pineapple juice, unsweetened
1 T.	cornstarch
1 T.	water
1	tomato, cut into 12 wedges
1	green pepper, cut into 12 wedges

NUTRITIONAL ANALYSIS

Calories: 255
Total fat: 7 g
Saturated fat: 1 g
% calories fat: 23
Carbohydrates: 22 g
Protein: 27 g
Cholesterol: 73 mg
Sodium: 252 mg

Cut the chicken into 1-inch cubes and place in a shallow glass pan. In a small bowl combine the lemon juice with pepper and pour over the breasts, turning to coat evenly. Cover tightly with plastic wrap and refrigerate 2–4 hours. Place the chicken on the skewers, following the Owner's Manual directions. Set the Timer for 15–20 minutes and cook at 425°F. The chicken is done when the juices run clear and there is no pink color visible. Discard remaining marinade. In a small saucepan combine oil, vinegar, sugar, ketchup and juice and heat through. Mix the cornstarch with the water and slowly pour into the sauce. Cook until the sauce is thick and clear. Add the tomato and green pepper, cooking for 2 minutes. Remove the chicken from the skewers and combine with the sauce. Serve immediately over steamed rice. Serves 4.

East Indian Chicken Kebabs

Ground coriander, chili powder and fresh ginger can all be found in your neighborhood supermarket.

4	boneless, skinless chicken breast halves
1 T.	olive oil
1 c.	plain lowfat yogurt
1 t.	chili powder
1 t.	ground coriander
3 T.	lemon juice
2 T.	minced garlic
2 t.	minced fresh ginger

NUTRITIONAL ANALYSIS

Calories:	363
Total fat:	10 g
Saturated fat:	3 g
% calories fat:	26
Carbohydrates:	6 g
Protein:	59 g
Cholesterol:	150 mg
Sodium:	170 mg

Cut the chicken into 1-inch cubes and place in a shallow glass pan. Combine all remaining ingredients in a small bowl and pour over the chicken cubes, turning the cubes to coat evenly. Tightly cover with plastic wrap and marinate for 4–12 hours. Thread the chicken on the skewers, following the Owner's Manual directions. Set the Timer for 15–20 minutes and cook at 425°F. The chicken is done when the juices run clear and there is no pink color visible. Discard remaining marinade. Serves 4.

Chicken & Two Pepper Pasta

The combination of red and green peppers and black olives gives this a beautiful presentation.

1	small onion, chopped
2	minced garlic cloves
1 t.	olive oil
8 oz.	vermicelli pasta, uncooked
2	boneless, skinless chicken breast halves
1	medium red pepper, chopped
1	medium green pepper, chopped
1/2 c.	sliced black olives
1/4 t.	salt
1/4 t.	pepper

NUTRITIONAL ANALYSIS

Calories:	414
Total fat:	7 g
Saturated fat:	1 g
% calories fat:	15
Carbohydrates:	50 g
Protein:	36 g
Cholesterol:	73 mg
Sodium:	354 mg

Place the chicken breasts in the adjustable basket of the rotisserie as directed in the Owner's Manual. Set the Timer for 15 minutes and cook at 425°F. Cool and chop. In a large pot, bring 3 quarts of water to a boil. Add vermicelli pasta, and cook 7 minutes or until tender. Meanwhile, in a medium nonstick pan, lightly sauté the onion and garlic in the olive oil. Add the red and green peppers, olives, salt and pepper and heat for 3 minutes. Add the chopped chicken. Drain the pasta and toss with chicken and pepper mixture. Serve immediately. Serves 4.

Dippin' Chicken with AirBaked Parsley Potatoes

This recipe is oh-so-easy and children absolutely love it.

1 lb.	potatoes, washed and cut into $1/2$-inch strips
1 t.	dried parsley
1 t.	garlic powder
4	boneless, skinless chicken breast halves
$1/2$ t.	salt
$1/2$ t.	pepper
$1/2$ t.	garlic salt
$1/2$ c.	hickory smoke barbecue sauce
$1/2$ c.	lowfat ranch dressing

NUTRITIONAL ANALYSIS

Calories:	470
Total fat:	7 g
Saturated fat:	2 g
% calories fat:	15
Carbohydrates:	38 g
Protein:	57 g
Cholesterol:	146 mg
Sodium:	1351 mg

Sprinkle the potatoes with the parsley and garlic powder. Place the potatoes in the roasted veggie/air bake basket, following the Owner's Manual directions. Set the Timer for 45 minutes and cook at 425°F. Remove the potatoes from the basket and place on a heatproof platter in a warm oven (200°F). Cut the chicken breasts into $1/2$-inch thick slices. Thread the chicken onto the skewers and season with the salt, pepper and garlic salt. Set the Timer for 15 minutes and cook at 425°F. The chicken is done when the juices run clear and there is no pink color visible. Arrange the chicken and potatoes on a serving platter and offer barbecue sauce and ranch dressing for "dippin." Serve with a chilled green salad. Serves 4.

Aunt Tia's Chicken Enchiladas

South of the Border flavor—new and improved!

3	boneless, skinless chicken breast halves
12	8-inch corn tortillas
2	14 oz. cans lowfat cream of chicken condensed soup
1	4 oz. can chopped green chiles, drained
2 c.	fat-free sour cream
1/2 c.	chopped green onion
1 c.	lowfat Monterey jack cheese

NUTRITIONAL ANALYSIS

Calories:	498
Total fat:	10 g
Saturated fat:	4 g
% calories fat:	18
Carbohydrates:	55 g
Protein:	43 g
Cholesterol:	104 mg
Sodium:	941 mg

Place the chicken in the adjustable basket as directed in the Owner's Manual. Set the Timer for 15 minutes and cook at 425°F. Cool and shred the chicken. To soften tortillas, spread and overlap the tortillas on the rotisserie baking sheet. Set the Timer for 8 minutes and cook at 425°F or until soft. Remove the tortillas from the oven and cover with plastic wrap. In a medium saucepan combine soup and green chiles. Heat and stir thoroughly. Add the sour cream and mix well. To assemble the enchiladas, lightly spray a 9" x 13" glass pan with vegetable spray. Fill each tortilla with a small amount of chicken, green onion and sour cream sauce and roll to close. Lay each filled tortilla in the glass pan and cover the enchiladas with remaining sauce. Top all with the cheese. Cover the enchiladas with aluminum foil. Place the wire rack on the lower shelf position of the rotisserie and put the enchiladas on the rack. Set the Timer for 45 minutes and cook at 425°F. Serves 6.

Tandoori Chicken

Citrus and spice combine to make this exotic chicken favorite.

4	boneless, skinless chicken breast halves
1/4 c.	lime juice
1/4 c.	lemon juice
1	small onion, chopped
2 T.	chopped garlic
1/2 t.	ground coriander
1/2 t.	turmeric
1/2 t.	ground cloves
1/4 t.	salt
1/4 t.	black pepper
2 t.	paprika
1 t.	fresh minced ginger
2 T.	chili powder
1 c.	plain nonfat yogurt

NUTRITIONAL ANALYSIS

Calories: 354
Total fat: 7 g
Saturated fat: 2 g
% calories fat: 18
Carbohydrates: 14 g
Protein: 59 g
Cholesterol: 147 mg
Sodium: 340 mg

Place the chicken in a shallow glass pan. Combine the juices and remaining ingredients in a small bowl. Pour over the chicken and seal tightly with plastic wrap. Refrigerate 4–12 hours. Place the chicken in the adjustable basket of the rotisserie, following the Owner's Manual directions. Set the Timer for 15 minutes and cook at 425°F. The chicken is done when the juices run clear and there is no pink color visible. Discard any remaining marinade. Serves 4.

Garlic Rotisserie Chicken

Assemble this rub mixture in the morning and refrigerate the chicken during the day. At dinnertime, you'll only need about 20 minutes to put this entrée on the table!

4	boneless, skinless chicken breast halves
$1/2$ c.	chopped cilantro
2 T.	minced garlic
1 t.	salt
$1/2$ t.	black pepper
1 T.	lime juice

NUTRITIONAL ANALYSIS	
Calories:	292
Total fat:	6 g
Saturated fat:	2 g
% calories fat:	19
Carbohydrates:	1 g
Protein:	55 g
Cholesterol:	146 mg
Sodium:	702 mg

Mix the cilantro, garlic, salt, pepper and lime juice together thoroughly. Place chicken breasts in shallow glass pan and generously cover each breast with the herb and juice mixture. Cover the pan tightly with plastic wrap and refrigerate 6–8 hours. Place the chicken in the adjustable basket of the rotisserie as directed in the Owner's Manual. Set the Timer for 15 minutes and cook at 425°F. The chicken is done when the juices run clear and there is no pink color visible. Discard any remaining marinade. Serves 4.

Classic Turkey Linguine

A light meal for a summer evening.

1	1 lb. boneless, skinless turkey breast
1 t.	olive oil
1	small chopped onion
4 T.	minced garlic
1 c.	fat-free chicken broth
2 T.	flour
2 T.	chopped fresh parsley
1/2 t.	dried oregano
1/2 t.	salt
1/4 t.	black pepper
1/4 c.	lowfat grated Parmesan cheese
1 lb.	linguine pasta, cooked
1	medium tomato, cut into wedges

NUTRITIONAL ANALYSIS	
Calories:	268
Total fat:	3 g
Saturated fat:	<1 g
% calories fat:	10
Carbohydrates:	17 g
Protein:	41 g
Cholesterol:	111 mg
Sodium:	516 mg

Place the turkey breast in the adjustable basket of the rotisserie as directed in the Owner's Manual. Set the Timer for 25 minutes and cook at 425°F. Cool and chop the turkey into small pieces. In a large nonstick skillet, sauté the onions and garlic in the olive oil. Remove from the pan. Pour the broth into the pan and sprinkle the flour over it, stirring well over medium heat, until the sauce thickens. Stir in the parsley, oregano, salt, pepper, turkey, onion and garlic. Simmer for 5 minutes to heat all ingredients. Serve over the hot pasta, sprinkle with grated Parmesan and garnish with tomato wedges. Serves 4.

Mediterranean Chicken & Vegetable Kebabs

Add rice pilaf and you have an entire meal!

¼ c.	olive oil
3 t.	lemon juice
1 t.	dried oregano
1 T.	minced garlic
1 t.	ground cumin
1 t.	black pepper
4	skinless chicken breast halves, cut into 1-inch cubes
1	medium red pepper, cut into 1-inch cubes
1	medium green pepper, cut into 1-inch cubes
1	small white onion, cut into large chunks
	prepared rice pilaf

NUTRITIONAL ANALYSIS

Calories: 432
Total fat: 19 g
Saturated fat: 3 g
% calories fat: 41
Carbohydrates: 6 g
Protein: 56 g
Cholesterol: 146 mg
Sodium: 122 mg

In a small bowl combine oil, juice, oregano, garlic, cumin and pepper. Place the chicken cubes in a shallow glass pan and pour the marinade over the chicken, turning to coat evenly. Tightly cover the pan with plastic wrap and refrigerate 4–8 hours. Thread the chicken cubes on the metal skewers, alternating the chicken with red and green peppers and onions. Discard remaining marinade. Place the skewers in the rotisserie as directed by the Owner's Manual. Set the Timer for 25–30 minutes and cook at 425°F. The chicken is done when the juices run clear and there is no pink color visible. Remove the chicken and vegetables from the skewers and serve with rice pilaf. Serves 4.

South of the Border Lasagna

Some assembly required—but it's worth it!

2	boneless, skinless chicken breast halves
1	small chopped onion
1	chopped green pepper
1 T.	chili powder
1/4 c.	chopped fresh cilantro
12	corn tortillas
2	10 oz. cans enchilada sauce
1	16 oz. can lowfat refried beans
1 c.	sliced black olives
2 c.	lowfat cheddar cheese, grated

NUTRITIONAL ANALYSIS	
Calories:	329
Total fat:	9 g
Saturated fat:	2 g
% calories fat:	25
Carbohydrates:	34 g
Protein:	28 g
Cholesterol:	43 mg
Sodium:	1137 mg

Place the chicken in the adjustable basket as directed in the Owner's Manual. Set the Timer for 15 minutes and cook at 425°F. Cool and shred the chicken. In a small bowl, mix together onion, green pepper, chili powder and cilantro. Lightly spray a 9" x 13" baking dish with vegetable spray. To assemble lasagna, spread a small amount of enchilada sauce on the bottom of the pan. Cover with tortillas (tear to loosely fit the pan), and additional sauce. Layer refried beans, chicken, onions and peppers, olives and cheese. Repeat layers, alternating ingredients. Sprinkle cheese on the top and cover with aluminum foil. Place the wire rack in the rotisserie on the lower shelf position. Put the enchiladas on the wire rack. Set the Timer for 45 minutes and cook at 425°F. Serves 8.

Spicy Chicken Thai Noodles

A satisfying and crunchy super quick entrée.

2	boneless, skinless chicken breast halves
8 oz.	thin vermicelli pasta
$1/4$ c.	chopped green onion
1 c.	fresh bean sprouts, washed
$1/2$	chopped red pepper
$1/4$ c.	chopped fresh cilantro

Dressing:

$1/2$ c.	water
$1/4$ c.	cider vinegar
$1/4$ c.	soy sauce
$1/4$ c.	fat-reduced peanut butter
2 t.	sesame (or vegetable) oil
1 T.	minced garlic
1 t.	brown sugar

NUTRITIONAL ANALYSIS	
Calories:	489
Total fat:	12 g
Saturated fat:	2 g
% calories fat:	22
Carbohydrates:	55 g
Protein:	41 g
Cholesterol:	73 mg
Sodium:	1183 mg

Place the chicken in the adjustable basket of the rotisserie as directed in the Owner's Manual. Set the Timer and cook for 15 minutes at 425°F. Cool and chop in small pieces. In a large pot, bring 3 quarts of water to a boil. Add the vermicelli pasta and cook 7 minutes or until tender. Drain the noodles and keep warm. Combine the cooked noodles with the chicken, onions, sprouts, red pepper and cilantro. Mix all the remaining ingredients for the dressing in a small bowl and blend well. Toss the dressing into the chicken and noodles and chill for 15–30 minutes. Serves 4.

Barbecued Chicken Pizza

Fast, fast, fast!

2	boneless, skinless chicken breast halves
1	14-inch prepared pizza crust
1/4 c.	barbecue sauce
2 c.	shredded lowfat mozzarella cheese
1 t.	dried Italian seasoning
1/2 t.	salt
1/4 t.	black pepper

NUTRITIONAL ANALYSIS

Calories:	302
Total fat:	9 g
Saturated fat:	3 g
% calories fat:	27
Carbohydrates:	22 g
Protein:	32 g
Cholesterol:	56 mg
Sodium:	717 mg

Place the chicken breasts into the adjustable basket of the rotisserie as directed by the Owner's Manual. Set the Timer for 15 minutes and cook at 425°F. Cool and shred the chicken. Place the pizza crust on the rotisserie baking sheet. Spread a layer of barbecue sauce over the crust. Sprinkle the cheese over the sauce and top with the shredded chicken. Lightly sprinkle Italian seasoning, salt and pepper over the pizza. Set the Timer for 15–20 minutes and bake at 450°F. Serves 6.

Gourmet Chicken & Garlic Pizza

This sophisticated pizza is fast becoming a national favorite. And, now, it's also lowfat!

2	boneless, skinless chicken breast halves
2 T.	minced garlic
1 t.	lowfat butter
1/4 c.	part-skin ricotta cheese
1/4 c.	lowfat plain yogurt
1/4 c.	lowfat grated Parmesan cheese
1/2 t.	cornstarch
1 t.	salt
1/2 t.	black pepper
1 T.	chopped fresh parsley
1	14-inch prepared pizza crust
1/2 c.	sliced black olives
1 c.	sliced fresh mushrooms
1/2 c.	lowfat grated Parmesan cheese

NUTRITIONAL ANALYSIS

Calories:	169
Total fat:	6 g
Saturated fat:	2 g
% calories fat:	30
Carbohydrates:	3 g
Protein:	26 g
Cholesterol:	62 mg
Sodium:	783 mg

Place the chicken breasts in the adjustable basket of the rotisserie as directed in the Owner's Manual. Set the Timer for 15 minutes and cook at 425°F. Cool and shred into small pieces. In a medium saucepan, lightly sauté the garlic cloves in butter until tender. Add the ricotta, yogurt and Parmesan cheese and mix well over low heat. Sprinkle the cornstarch into the sauce and stir constantly, until the sauce thickens slightly. Add salt, pepper, chicken and parsley. Place the pizza crust on the rotisserie baking sheet. Spoon the sauce onto the prepared crust and top with the olives, mushrooms and Parmesan cheese. Set the Timer for 15–20 minutes and bake at 450°F. Serves 6.

Quick Turkey Burgers

A healthful alternative to traditional burgers. Serve with all your favorite condiments.

1 lb.	ground turkey
1/4 c.	finely chopped onion
1/4 c.	finely chopped green pepper
1/4 c.	shredded lowfat cheddar cheese
2 t.	Worcestershire sauce
1/4 t.	black pepper
1/2 t.	salt
4	hamburger buns

NUTRITIONAL ANALYSIS

Calories:	332
Total fat:	13 g
Saturated fat:	4 g
% calories fat:	37
Carbohydrates:	24 g
Protein:	28 g
Cholesterol:	84 mg
Sodium:	689 mg

In a large bowl, mix together turkey, onion, green pepper, cheese, Worcestershire sauce, pepper and salt. Shape into four patties of equal thickness. Place the turkey patties in the adjustable basket, following the Owner's Manual directions. Set the Timer for 15 minutes and cook at 450°F. Serve with fat-free mayonnaise, mustard, sweet red onion slices, pickles or other favorite condiments. Serves 4.

Barbecue Chicken Sandwiches

Homemade BBQ for a Sunday evening treat!

3	boneless, skinless chicken breast halves
6	onion rolls, split

Sauce:

1 t.	vegetable oil
1	small minced onion
1 c.	tomato sauce
3/4 c.	ketchup
1/4 c.	brown sugar
1/4 c.	cider vinegar
2 T.	molasses
1 T.	Dijon mustard
1 T.	chili sauce

NUTRITIONAL ANALYSIS	
Calories:	397
Total fat:	7 g
Saturated fat:	2 g
% calories fat:	16
Carbohydrates:	50g
Protein:	34 g
Cholesterol:	73 mg
Sodium:	1046 mg

Place the chicken in the adjustable basket of the rotisserie as directed in the Owner's Manual. Set the Timer for 15 minutes and cook at 425°F. Cool and shred the chicken. In a medium nonstick pan, sauté the onions in the oil until tender. Blend in the remaining sauce ingredients and simmer for 10 minutes. Add the cooked chicken and simmer for 2 minutes or until heated through. To serve, scoop barbecued chicken meat onto each onion roll half. Top with tomatoes, pickles and onions, if desired. Serves 6.

New Orleans Chicken Gumbo

Perfect for a winter evening!

3	boneless, skinless chicken breast halves
1/2 c.	lowfat cooked ham, diced
1/2 t.	Cajun spice
1	14 1/2 oz. can stewed tomatoes
1	14 1/2 oz. can fat-free chicken broth
1/4 c.	chopped onion
1/2 c.	frozen okra, cut
1 c.	chopped celery
1/2 c.	chopped green pepper
1 T.	minced garlic
2 c.	water
3/4 c.	instant rice
1 t.	salt
1/2 t.	black pepper

NUTRITIONAL ANALYSIS	
Calories:	279
Total fat:	5 g
Saturated fat:	1 g
% calories fat:	17
Carbohydrates:	23 g
Protein:	34 g
Cholesterol:	77 mg
Sodium:	1032 mg

Place the chicken in the adjustable basket of the rotisserie as directed in the Owner's Manual. Set the Timer for 15 minutes and cook at 425°F. Cool and chop the chicken into small pieces. In a large cooking pot, combine the chicken and all remaining ingredients in the order given. Adjust salt and pepper to taste. Simmer approximately 20–30 minutes to allow the flavors to develop. Ladle into bowls. Serves 6.

Chapter 6

Flavorful Rotisserie Fish & Shellfish

Fish is an all-time favorite food, whether it comes from the West Coast, the East Coast or the shores of an icy-cold lake. The delicate texture and mild flavor of fish naturally lead to wonderful recipes, whether you bake it, poach it, fry it or grill it. And, because fish packs plenty of healthful protein and lower fat, you can prepare fish with confidence, knowing that you are giving your family the best of nutritious choices. In this chapter you'll find recipes for fish and shellfish that are designed to bring out the full flavors of the fish, rather than masking the flavor with a sauce or heavy spices.

A NOTE TO THE COOK

If you are a novice at preparing fish and shellfish, you should know that fish requires some care to prepare and serve it properly. But don't be scared away by the thought. Instead, follow these tips on buying, storing and preparing fish and then try the recipes in this chapter. You'll find that you'll want to serve fish often!

- To select whole, fresh fish look for bright, clear eyes and reddish-pink gills. The scales should be bright and shiny. Fresh fish doesn't have a "fishy" odor and the flesh should be firm.

- The definitions for various cuts of fish can be confusing. For example, "whole" fish means that it is just as it comes from the water. The term "dressed" means that the fish has been cleaned (eviscerated), scaled and the head, tail and fins have been removed. "Steaks" refer to large dressed fish and are usually about ¾-inch thick. The "fillets" are from the sides of the fish, have few or no bones and are cut lengthwise away from the backbone.

- Fish and shellfish are widely available frozen. If you purchase it frozen, keep it frozen until you use it. If you purchase it fresh, use it within two days.

- The most important rule about fish is not to overcook it. Fish cooks very quickly, so watch the cooking process carefully. Fish will flake easily when cooked. It shouldn't be dry-looking.

- There are two types of fish, referred to as either "fatty" or "lean." Fatty fish includes those that have more distinct flavors, such as salmon, tuna, mackerel, catfish and butterfish. The lean type includes fish such as sole, mahi-mahi, orange roughy and flounder.

- After cooking fish, refrigerate any leftovers and eat it within a day.

① FISH: STEAKS, FILLETS & DELICATE DISHES

Try a variety of different types of fish in the following recipes. You can make substitutions as long as you are aware of the fat content of the fish you've selected.

Swordfish Rotisserie Steaks

Try serving this with Broccoli Risotto (p. 181), on a special evening.

4	6 oz. swordfish steaks, ³/₄-inch thick	
1 c.	lowfat buttermilk	
1 t.	tabasco sauce	

NUTRITIONAL ANALYSIS	
Calories:	168
Total fat:	5 g
Saturated fat:	2 g
% calories fat:	29
Carbohydrates:	3 g
Protein:	25 g
Cholesterol:	49 mg
Sodium:	177 mg

Place the steaks in a shallow glass pan. Combine the buttermilk and tabasco and pour over the steaks. Turn the steaks to coat evenly. Cover the fish with plastic wrap and refrigerate for 2 hours. Drain the fish and pat dry with paper towels. Place the fish in the adjustable basket of the rotisserie as directed in the Owner's Manual. Set the Timer for 15–20 minutes and cook at 450°F. The fish will flake easily when done. Serves 4.

Orange Red Snapper

This rich, mild-flavored fish is a delight to serve.

1	1 lb. red snapper fillets
1/4 c.	orange juice
1 T.	vegetable oil
1 t.	soy sauce
1/4 t.	minced fresh ginger
1/4 t.	pepper
1 T.	minced garlic
1 T.	lemon juice

NUTRITIONAL ANALYSIS	
Calories:	186
Total fat:	5 g
Saturated fat:	1 g
% calories fat:	27
Carbohydrates:	2 g
Protein:	30 g
Cholesterol:	53 mg
Sodium:	151 mg

Place the fillets in a shallow glass pan. Combine the juice, oil, soy sauce, ginger, pepper and garlic in a small bowl. Pour over the fillets. Turn the fillets to coat evenly. Cover the fish with plastic wrap and refrigerate for 2 hours. Drain the fish and discard the marinade. Place the fish in the adjustable basket of the rotisserie as directed in the Owner's Manual. Set the Timer for 15–18 minutes and cook at 450°F. The fish will flake easily when done. Drizzle the lemon juice over the fish just before serving. Serves 4.

Dill Salmon

Delicate herbs baste the fish.

2 T.	lowfat margarine
1 T.	chopped fresh parsley
2 T.	chopped fresh dill
1/4 c.	fat-free mayonnaise
2 t.	nonfat milk
1 t.	pepper
1/2 t.	salt
4	6 oz. salmon steaks, 1-inch thick

NUTRITIONAL ANALYSIS

Calories:	331
Total fat:	15 g
Saturated fat:	3 g
% calories fat:	41
Carbohydrates:	4 g
Protein:	44 g
Cholesterol:	107 mg
Sodium:	562 mg

Combine the margarine, parsley, dill, mayonnaise, milk, pepper and salt in a small bowl. Mix well. Brush the salmon steaks on both sides with the sauce. Place the fish in the adjustable basket as directed in the Owner's Manual. Set the Timer for 15–20 minutes and cook at 450°F. The fish will flake easily when done. Serves 4.

Orange Roughy with Pineapple Salsa

The fruit flavors impeccably complement the orange roughy.

1	1 lb. orange roughy fillets
1/4 t.	pepper
1 c.	chopped fresh pineapple
2 T.	orange juice concentrate, undiluted
1/4 c.	chopped red onion
1/4 c.	chopped fresh cilantro
2 T.	lime juice
1/4 t.	salt

NUTRITIONAL ANALYSIS

Calories:	139
Total fat:	1 g
Saturated fat:	<1 g
% calories fat:	8
Carbohydrates:	10 g
Protein:	22 g
Cholesterol:	29 mg
Sodium:	238 mg

Place the fillets into the adjustable basket of the rotisserie as directed in the Owner's Manual. Sprinkle the pepper over the fish. Set the Timer for 15–18 minutes and cook at 450°F. The fish will flake easily when done. In a small serving bowl, combine the pineapple, orange juice, onion, cilantro, lime juice and salt. Mix gently. Serve the salsa aside the fillets. Serves 4.

Garlic Grilled Salmon

Perfectly grilled salmon is flaky and tender.

4	4 oz. salmon steaks, 1-inch thick
2 T.	olive oil
1/4 c.	soy sauce
3 T.	lemon juice
1 T.	minced garlic
1/2 t.	dried basil
2 T.	lemon juice

NUTRITIONAL ANALYSIS	
Calories:	278
Total fat:	16 g
Saturated fat:	3 g
% calories fat:	53
Carbohydrates:	4 g
Protein:	29 g
Cholesterol:	71 mg
Sodium:	1088 mg

Place the steaks in a shallow glass pan. Combine the oil, soy sauce, lemon juice, garlic and basil in a small bowl. Pour over the steaks. Turn the steaks to coat evenly. Cover the fish with plastic wrap and refrigerate for 2–4 hours. Drain the fish and discard the marinade. Place the fish in the adjustable basket of the rotisserie as directed in the Owner's Manual. Set the Timer for 15–20 minutes and cook at 450°F. The fish will flake easily when done. Drizzle the lemon juice over the fish just before serving. Serves 4.

Ahi Tuna Kebabs

A healthful entrée for any night.

1 lb.	ahi tuna, cut into 1-inch pieces
2 T.	olive oil
1/2 c.	clam juice
1/4 c.	red wine vinegar
2 T.	garlic
1 T.	fresh chopped basil
1/2 t.	pepper
12	small red tomatoes
12	small mushrooms
1	red onion, cut into chunks

NUTRITIONAL ANALYSIS

Calories:	315
Total fat:	9 g
Saturated fat:	1 g
% calories fat:	26
Carbohydrates:	22 g
Protein:	39 g
Cholesterol:	66 mg
Sodium:	204 mg

Place the tuna pieces in a shallow glass pan. Combine the oil, clam juice, vinegar, garlic, basil and pepper and pour over the tuna. Cover and marinate for 1 hour in the refrigerator. Thread the tuna, tomatoes, mushrooms and onion on the skewers, alternating each. Place the kebabs in the rotisserie as directed by the Owner's Manual. Set the Timer for 20–25 minutes and cook at 450°F. Serves 4.

Brazilian Red Snapper

The citrus juices gives this snapper an exciting taste!

4	6 oz. red snapper fillets
1/2 c.	lime juice
1/4 c.	orange juice concentrate, undiluted
1 T.	olive oil
1 T.	minced garlic
1 T.	chopped fresh parsley
1 T.	fresh lemon juice

NUTRITIONAL ANALYSIS	
Calories:	287
Total fat:	6 g
Saturated fat:	1 g
% calories fat:	21
Carbohydrates:	10 g
Protein:	45 g
Cholesterol:	80 mg
Sodium:	98 mg

Place the fillets in a shallow glass pan. Combine the lime juice, orange juice concentrate, oil, garlic and parsley in a small bowl. Pour over the fillets. Turn the fillets to coat evenly. Cover the fish with plastic wrap and refrigerate for 2–4 hours. Drain the fish and discard the marinade. Place the fish in the adjustable basket of the rotisserie as directed in the Owner's Manual. Set the Timer for 15–18 minutes and cook at 450ºF. The fish will flake easily when done. Drizzle the lemon juice over the fish just before serving. Serves 4.

Mustard-Lime Ahi Tuna

The tart and tangy marinade fully develops the flavor of the tuna.

4	6 oz. tuna fillets
1/4 c.	fresh lime juice
2 t.	Dijon mustard
1 T.	olive oil
1 T.	minced garlic
1 T.	soy sauce
1/2 t.	ground ginger
1/4 t.	salt
1/4 t.	pepper

NUTRITIONAL ANALYSIS	
Calories:	279
Total fat:	6 g
Saturated fat:	<1 g
% calories fat:	19
Carbohydrates:	33 g
Protein:	52g
Cholesterol:	99 mg
Sodium:	546 mg

Place the fillets in a shallow glass pan. Combine the juice, mustard, oil, garlic, soy sauce, ginger, salt and pepper and mix well. Pour the marinade over the fillets, cover tightly and refrigerate for 2–4 hours. Place the fish in the adjustable basket as directed in the Owner's Manual. Discard any remaining marinade. Set the Timer for 15–20 minutes and cook at 450°F. The tuna will flake easily when done. Serves 4.

California Fish Tacos

A favorite for the whole family!

1	1 lb. swordfish fillet, cut into 1-inch pieces
$1/2$ c.	fresh lime juice
$1/2$ t.	chili pepper
	non-stick cooking spray
12	8-inch corn tortillas
2 c.	shredded lettuce
1 c.	diced tomatoes
$1/4$ c.	chopped red onion
$1/2$ c.	shredded lowfat Monterey jack cheese

NUTRITIONAL ANALYSIS	
Calories:	277
Total fat:	7 g
Saturated fat:	2 g
% calories fat:	23
Carbohydrates:	29 g
Protein:	26 g
Cholesterol:	43 mg
Sodium:	249 mg

Place the fillet pieces in a shallow glass pan. Combine the lime juice and pepper and brush over the fillets. Turn the fillets to coat evenly. Cover the fish with plastic wrap and refrigerate for 2–4 hours. Drain the fish. Place the fish in the adjustable basket of the rotisserie as directed in the Owner's Manual. Set the Timer for 15–20 minutes and cook at 450°F. The fish will flake easily when done. Lightly coat the rotisserie baking sheet with the cooking spray and place four tortillas on it. Set the Timer for 15 minutes and cook at 425°F. The tortillas should be crisp. Repeat with the remaining tortillas. Assemble fish, tortillas, lettuce, tomatoes, onion and cheese and invite everyone to build their own tacos. Serves 6.

Herbed Halibut

These subtle herbs create an excellent marinade for the halibut.

4	6 oz. halibut steaks, 1-inch thick
1/4 c.	chopped green onion
2 T.	minced garlic
1 T.	dried thyme
1 T.	dried basil
2 T.	olive oil
1/2 c.	fat-free chicken broth
1 t.	pepper

NUTRITIONAL ANALYSIS	
Calories:	315
Total fat:	12 g
Saturated fat:	2 g
% calories fat:	35
Carbohydrates:	3 g
Protein:	47 g
Cholesterol:	70 mg
Sodium:	142 mg

Place the steaks in a shallow glass pan. In a small bowl, combine the onion, garlic, thyme, basil, oil, broth and pepper. Pour over the steaks and turn the fillets to coat evenly. Cover the fish with plastic wrap and refrigerate for 2–4 hours. Drain the fish and discard the marinade. Place the fish in the adjustable basket of the rotisserie as directed in the Owner's Manual. Set the Timer for 15–20 minutes and cook at 450°F. The fish will flake easily when done. Serves 4.

Paprika Mahi-Mahi Fillets

The delicate flavor of this fish goes well with the herbed butter sauce.

4	6 oz. mahi-mahi fillets
1 t.	pepper
1/2 t.	paprika
2 T.	lowfat margarine, softened
1 T.	minced fresh parsley
1 T.	minced garlic

NUTRITIONAL ANALYSIS	
Calories:	175
Total fat:	4 g
Saturated fat:	<1 g
% calories fat:	22
Carbohydrates:	1 g
Protein:	32 g
Cholesterol:	124 mg
Sodium:	189 mg

Place the fish steaks in the adjustable basket of the rotisserie as directed in the Owner's Manual. Set the Timer for 15–18 minutes and cook at 450°F. The fish will flake easily when done. Mix all the remaining ingredients in a small bowl and brush each cooked fillet with the herbed butter. Serves 4.

Red Tomato & Pepper Whitefish

A colorful salsa accompanies the fish.

1	1 lb. whitefish fillet
1/4 c.	fresh lime juice
1/2 t.	salt
1 T.	olive oil
1	chopped onion
1	chopped green pepper
1 T.	minced garlic
2 c.	chopped tomatoes
1/2	jalapeno pepper, seeded and minced
1/2 t.	pepper

NUTRITIONAL ANALYSIS	
Calories:	223
Total fat:	11 g
Saturated fat:	2 g
% calories fat:	42
Carbohydrates:	9 g
Protein:	24 g
Cholesterol:	70 mg
Sodium:	359 mg

Place the fish in the adjustable basket of the rotisserie as directed in the Owner's Manual. Set the Timer for 15–20 minutes and cook at 450°F. The fish will flake easily when done. While the fish is cooking, prepare the salsa by combining the remaining ingredients. Top each piece of fish with a heaping tablespoon of the salsa and serve the remaining salsa on the side. Serves 4.

Honey-Roasted Salmon

The tangy sweetness of this marinade accents the salmon beautifully.

4	4 oz. salmon fillets
1/4 c.	Dijon mustard
2 T.	lowfat margarine, softened
2 T.	honey
2 t.	chopped parsley
1/2 t.	salt
1/4 t.	pepper

NUTRITIONAL ANALYSIS	
Calories:	279
Total fat:	13 g
Saturated fat:	3 g
% calories fat:	44
Carbohydrates:	11 g
Protein:	29 g
Cholesterol:	71 mg
Sodium:	767 mg

Place the fish in the adjustable basket of the rotisserie as directed in the Owner's Manual. Set the Timer for 15–20 minutes and cook at 450°F. The fish will flake easily when done. While the fish is cooking, prepare the sauce by combining the remaining ingredients. Blend well. Drizzle the honey sauce over each fillet just before serving. Serves 4.

Pesto & Tomato Shark Fillets

Robust Italian flavors fully enhance this fish.

1	1 lb. shark fillet
1 c.	chopped tomato
1 T.	olive oil
1 t.	pepper
½ t.	salt
½ c.	prepared pesto
¼ c.	lowfat grated Parmesan cheese

NUTRITIONAL ANALYSIS

Calories:	257
Total fat:	12 g
Saturated fat:	2 g
% calories fat:	41
Carbohydrates:	5 g
Protein:	32 g
Cholesterol:	56 mg
Sodium:	654 mg

Place the fish in the adjustable basket of the rotisserie as directed in the Owner's Manual. Set the Timer for 15–20 minutes and cook at 450°F. The fish will flake easily when done. While the fish is cooking, prepare the sauce by combining the tomato, oil, pepper, salt and pesto. Blend well. Cover each fillet with the tomato-pesto sauce and top with Parmesan cheese. Serves 4.

Herb Roasted Fish Steaks

Use any lean-type fish for this recipe.

4	6 oz. fish steaks
1 T.	olive oil
$1/2$ t.	salt
$1/4$ t.	pepper
1 T.	chopped fresh parsley
$1/2$ t.	dried oregano
$1/2$ t.	dried basil
1	lemon, cut into wedges

NUTRITIONAL ANALYSIS	
Calories:	127
Total fat:	3 g
Saturated fat:	<1 g
% calories fat:	22
Carbohydrates:	2 g
Protein:	22 g
Cholesterol:	54 mg
Sodium:	255 mg

Place the fish in the adjustable basket of the rotisserie as directed in the Owner's Manual. Combine the oil, salt, pepper, parsley, oregano and basil in a small bowl and mix well. Brush the herb sauce over the fish. Set the Timer for 15–18 minutes and cook at 450°F. When the fish flakes easily, remove from the oven and brush with any remaining sauce. Serve with lemon wedges. Serves 6.

Lemon & Orange Mahi-Mahi

A citrus delight!

1/2 c.	orange juice concentrate
1/4 c.	fresh lemon juice
2 T.	olive oil
1 t.	pepper
1/2 t.	salt
2 T.	chopped fresh parsley
4	4 oz. mahi-mahi fillets

NUTRITIONAL ANALYSIS

Calories:	146
Total fat:	5 g
Saturated fat:	<1 g
% calories fat:	32
Carbohydrates:	10 g
Protein:	15 g
Cholesterol:	55 mg
Sodium:	262 mg

In a small bowl, combine the juices, oil, pepper, salt and parsley. Place the fillets in a shallow pan and pour the marinade over, turning the fish to coat evenly. Refrigerate for 2–4 hours. Place the fish in the adjustable basket of the rotisserie as directed in the Owner's Manual. Set the Timer for 15–18 minutes and cook at 450°F. Discard any remaining marinade. The fish will flake easily when done. Serves 4.

2 SHELLFISH: LIGHT & LOWFAT

Shellfish lovers agree that there are no better mild, rich flavors on earth than those found in shellfish. Because shellfish contain very little fat, you can enjoy the taste often!

Scallops & Vegetable Kebabs

A beautiful combination of fish and vegetables. Serve with steamed rice or hot pasta.

16	sea scallops
12	cherry tomatoes
1	small onion, cut into chunks
12	2-inch mushrooms
3 T.	lemon juice
2 T.	chopped fresh dill
1 T.	lowfat margarine, softened
1 T.	minced garlic
dash	paprika

NUTRITIONAL ANALYSIS

Calories:	95
Total fat:	3 g
Saturated fat:	<1 g
% calories fat:	28
Carbohydrates:	10 g
Protein:	9 g
Cholesterol:	13 mg
Sodium:	191 mg

Clean and rinse the scallops and pat dry. Thread the scallops, tomatoes, onions and mushrooms alternately on the skewers. In a small bowl, combine the juice, dill, margarine, garlic and paprika. Place the kebabs in the rotisserie as directed by the Owner's Manual. Brush the kebabs with the herb butter. Set the Timer for 20–25 minutes and cook at 450°F. Serves 4.

Hawaiian Rotisserie Jumbo Shrimp

Quick and easy for any night of the week.

1	1 lb. uncooked jumbo shrimp, peeled and deveined
1	16 oz. can unsweetened pineapple chunks, drained
1/4 c.	orange juice
2 T.	lime juice
1 T.	vegetable oil
1 T.	Worcestershire sauce

NUTRITIONAL ANALYSIS	
Calories:	180
Total fat:	5 g
Saturated fat:	<1 g
% calories fat:	24
Carbohydrates:	17 g
Protein:	18 g
Cholesterol:	161 mg
Sodium:	228 mg

Place the shrimp in a shallow glass pan. Combine the pineapple, juices, oil and Worcestershire sauce and pour over the shrimp. Cover and marinate for 1 hour in the refrigerator. Thread the shrimp and the pineapple on the skewers, alternating each. Place the kebabs in the rotisserie as directed by the Owner's Manual.

Brush the kebabs with the marinade again. Set the Timer for 15–20 minutes and cook at 450°F. Serves 4.

Hot & Spicy Jumbo Shrimp

Serve with AirBaked Onion Potatoes (p. 53).

2 lbs.	uncooked jumbo shrimp, peeled and deveined
2 T.	minced parsley
2 T.	olive oil
2 T.	Worcestershire sauce
$1/4$ l.	hot pepper sauce
$1/4$ c.	chili pepper
2 T.	minced garlic
1 t.	salt
$1/2$ t.	pepper
$1/4$ c.	cider vinegar

NUTRITIONAL ANALYSIS

Calories: 160
Total fat: 6 g
Saturated fat: <1 g
% calories fat: 33
Carbohydrates: 3 g
Protein: 23 g
Cholesterol: 215 mg
Sodium: 692 mg

Place the shrimp in a shallow glass pan. Combine the parsley, oil, Worcestershire sauce, hot pepper sauce, chili pepper, garlic, salt, pepper, and vinegar and pour over the shrimp. Cover and marinate for 1 hour in the refrigerator. Place the shrimp on the skewers as directed in the Owner's Manual. Set the Timer for 20 minutes and cook at 450°F. Serves 6.

Chapter 7

All the Accompaniments: Vegetables, Salads, Desserts & More

Here are the perfect accompaniments for your meals! Each recipe is designed to be creative, healthful and, of course, absolutely delicious. With choices like Grilled Chicken Caesar Salad, Herbed Polenta and Fresh Boysenberry Cobbler, you will find new taste combinations and lowfat versions of many favorites. And, with the roasted veggie/air bake basket and the oven baking sheet, your rotisserie can quickly adapt to a wide variety of uses. Whether you are roasting, grilling or baking in your rotisserie, you'll find that these recipes fit your busy, everyday lifestyle.

A NOTE TO THE COOK

Here are some easy ways to organize, plan and prepare your meals:

- Always shop with a list. We've been told this for years and it's still true! We live super-busy lives these days, but taking the time to plan your shopping list really pays off. When you shop from your list you won't have to make all those extra "quick trips" to the store every other day and, just as importantly, you won't buy what you don't need.

- Before you start preparing a meal, think about the timing of each recipe. Start with the food that takes the longest to prepare and work forward from there. In fact, think about tomorrow's recipes today. Marinate a roast or chicken tonight for your dinner tomorrow. The more you focus on organizing your meals, the easier your preparations will be.

- Cook, chop, slice and dice more food than you need. If you are going to rotisserie a chicken, cook two instead. You'll be able to save the cooked chicken meat for another recipe during the week. If you are chopping something you commonly prepare, such as onions, chop twice as many as you need. You'll have them all ready to go for the next meal.

- Use containers that can go from the refrigerator to the oven and back to the freezer. Use plastic bags to mix ingredients, to marinate meat or poultry and to store small amounts of food. Line your heavy cooking pans with foil. Each of these shortcuts will help you avoid the tedious dishwashing routine.

- Since many of the nutrients of certain fruits and vegetables are in the skin, don't peel them unless you need to. Vegetables and fruits such as potatoes, carrots, cucumbers, nectarines, plums and apples are better left unpeeled.

- When you are caught short-handed on ingredients in the middle of a recipe, don't be afraid to try a substitution. For example, if you don't have molasses, try brown sugar. If you don't have lemon juice, try lime juice instead. You may be pleasantly surprised by the end results!

1 VEGETABLES: FROM THE GARDEN TO YOUR TABLE

Fresh vegetables practically burst with the goodness of natural vitamins and minerals. In this section George shares some of his favorite vegetable recipes that will offer you delicious flavors while maintaining those natural nutrients. You'll find the roasted veggie/air bake basket of your Big George rotisserie is especially handy for fresh vegetables because the basket gently roasts the vegetables in the constant movement of warm air. The results are tender, crisp vegetables prepared without any fat! And, many of these recipes, such as Zesty Parmesan Zucchini and Sweet Potato Fries, are also excellent snacks for any time of the day.

Italian Baby Potatoes

Marinate these potatoes early in the day and enjoy their robust flavor for dinner.

10	small, new potatoes, washed and halved
2 T.	olive oil
1/4 c.	cider vinegar
1 t.	Dijon mustard
1/2 t.	salt
1 T.	Italian seasoning
1/4 c.	finely chopped green onion
1/2 t.	pepper

NUTRITIONAL ANALYSIS	
Calories:	216
Total fat:	5 g
Saturated fat:	<1 g
% calories fat:	20
Carbohydrates:	41 g
Protein:	4 g
Cholesterol:	0 mg
Sodium:	251 mg

Place the potatoes in a shallow glass pan. Mix the remaining ingredients and pour over the potatoes. Turn the potatoes to coat evenly. Cover the potatoes with plastic wrap and refrigerate 6–12 hours. Place the potatoes in the roasted veggie/air bake basket as directed in the Owner's Manual. Set the Timer for 45 minutes and cook at 425°F. Serves 6.

Herbed Yukon Gold Potatoes

These buttery potatoes go well with almost any entrée. Because they are virtually fat-free, you can enjoy these flavors guilt-free, too!

6	Yukon Gold potatoes
1/2 t.	salt
1/2 t.	pepper
1 T.	fresh chopped parsley
1/2 t.	dried oregano

NUTRITIONAL ANALYSIS	
Calories:	96
Total fat:	<1 g
Saturated fat:	<1 g
% calories fat:	1
Carbohydrates:	23 g
Protein:	2 g
Cholesterol:	0 mg
Sodium:	382 mg

Cut the potatoes into ½-inch cubes and place them in the roasted veggie/air bake basket of the rotisserie as directed in the Owner's Manual. Set the Timer for 45 minutes and bake at 425°F. Place the cooked potatoes on a serving platter and toss with the spices and parsley. Serve while warm. Serves 6.

Rotisserie Onions & Mushrooms

An unusually elegant way to serve sweet onions.

2	medium sweet onions
1/2 c.	thinly sliced mushrooms
1/2 c.	fat-free beef broth
1/4 t.	pepper

Peel the onions, cut in half and place in the adjustable basket of the rotisserie as directed in the Owner's Manual. Set the Timer for 35 minutes and cook at 425°F. While the onions bake, mix together the mushrooms, broth and pepper. Heat in a small saucepan and simmer for 5 minutes. When the onions are cooked, remove from the basket and place 1 onion half in each individual bowl. Pour a small amount of the mushroom sauce over each serving. Serves 4.

Lemon & Herb Artichokes

These tender artichokes have a delicate, herb-flavored taste.

4	small artichokes
1/4 c.	lemon juice
2 T.	olive oil
2 T.	cider vinegar
1/4 t.	pepper
1 T.	Italian seasoning

NUTRITIONAL ANALYSIS

Calories:	122
Total fat:	7 g
Saturated fat:	<1 g
% calories fat:	43
Carbohydrates:	17 g
Protein:	4 g
Cholesterol:	0 mg
Sodium:	156 mg

Trim woody leaves and stems from the artichokes. Cut each artichoke in half. Pour the lemon juice into 2 quarts of cold water and soak the artichokes for 5 minutes. Mix together the olive oil, vinegar, pepper and Italian seasoning. Place the artichokes in the adjustable basket of the rotisserie as directed in the Owner's Manual. Set the Timer for 30 minutes and cook at 425°F. When cooked, place the artichokes on a serving platter and drizzle the oil and vinegar sauce into each of the halves. Serves 4.

Zesty Parmesan Zucchini

A delicious way to enjoy fresh zucchini!

4	medium zucchini, washed
2 T.	Parmesan cheese
1/2 t.	onion powder
1/4 t.	black pepper

NUTRITIONAL ANALYSIS	
Calories:	37
Total fat:	1 g
Saturated fat:	<1 g
% calories fat:	29
Carbohydrates:	4 g
Protein:	4g
Cholesterol:	2 mg
Sodium:	61 mg

Cut the zucchini into 2" x 1/2" strips and place in the roasted veggie/air bake basket as directed in the Owner's Manual. Set the Timer for 30 minutes and cook at 425°F. Zucchini should be tender-crisp. Place the zucchini in a serving bowl and toss with the Parmesan cheese, onion powder and pepper. Serves 4.

Sweet Potato Fries

Great flavor!

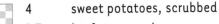

4	sweet potatoes, scrubbed
1 T.	lowfat margarine
2 t.	sugar
1 t.	cinnamon

NUTRITIONAL ANALYSIS

Calories:	117
Total fat:	1 g
Saturated fat:	<1 g
% calories fat:	11
Carbohydrates:	25 g
Protein:	2 g
Cholesterol:	0 mg
Sodium:	207 mg

Cut the sweet potatoes into ½-inch fries and place in the roasted veggie/air bake basket as directed in the Owner's Manual. Set the Timer for 45 minutes and cook at 425°F. Combine the sugar and cinnamon in a small bowl. When the potatoes are cooked, transfer them to a large bowl and toss with the sugar and cinnamon mixture. Serves 4.

Summer Vegetable Kebabs

Serve as a side dish or as a light luncheon entrée.

1	medium red pepper, cut into 1-inch pieces
2	ears of corn, sliced into 1-inch pieces
2	medium fresh zucchini, sliced into 1-inch pieces
1	medium red onion, cut into chunks
1/4 c.	lowfat margarine, softened
2 T.	minced green onion
2 T.	minced garlic
2 T.	minced fresh parsley
1 t.	garlic salt
1/2 t.	pepper

NUTRITIONAL ANALYSIS

Calories: 129

Total fat: 6 g

Saturated fat: 1 g

% calories fat: 41

Carbohydrates: 17 g

Protein: 3 g

Cholesterol: 0 mg

Sodium: 541 mg

Thread the pepper, corn, zucchini, and onion on the skewers, alternating vegetables. Combine the margarine and remaining ingredients and brush on the vegetables, turning to coat evenly. Place the skewers in the rotisserie, as directed in the Owner's Manual. Set the Timer for 25 minutes and cook at 450°F. Remove from the skewers and let cool for 5 minutes. Brush with any remaining herb butter. Serves 4.

Roasted Summer Squash

Delicate flavors enhance this buttery vegetable.

4   summer squash, washed
1 c.   fat-free Parmesan garlic salad dressing

Cut each squash in half lengthwise and place in a shallow glass pan. Pour the Parmesan garlic salad dressing over the squash and cover with plastic wrap. Refrigerate for 1–2 hours. Place the squash in the adjustable basket as directed in the Owner's Manual. Set the Timer for 35 minutes and cook at 425°F. Serves 4.

NUTRITIONAL ANALYSIS	
Calories:	49
Total fat:	<1 g
Saturated fat:	<1 g
% calories fat:	5
Carbohydrates:	8 g
Protein:	1 g
Cholesterol:	0 mg
Sodium:	562 mg

AirBaked Ranch Fries

Practically fat free and delicious!

8   potatoes, washed and sliced into $^1/_2$-inch strips
1 T.   dry ranch-flavored salad dressing mix

Toss the cut potatoes with the dry salad dressing mix.
Place the potatoes in the roasted veggie/air bake basket of
the rotisserie as directed in the Owner's Manual. Set the
Timer for 45 minutes and cook at 425°F. Serves 8.

NUTRITIONAL ANALYSIS	
Calories:	123
Total fat:	<1 g
Saturated fat:	<1 g
% calories fat:	1
Carbohydrates:	28 g
Protein:	3 g
Cholesterol:	0 mg
Sodium:	129 mg

Sweet & Tasty Snackin' Carrots

Carrots have a naturally sweet taste that is accentuated by the roasting process. Serve as a nonfat good-for-you vegetable anytime of day!

| 8 | medium carrots |
| dash | salt (optional) |

Cut the carrots into slices 2 inches in length and ½-inch thick. Place the carrots in the roasted veggie/air bake basket of the rotisserie as directed in the Owner's Manual. Set the Timer for 25–30 minutes and cook at 425°F. Cool and sprinkle with salt, if desired. Serves 4.

NUTRITIONAL ANALYSIS	
Calories:	62
Total fat:	<1 g
Saturated fat:	<1 g
% calories fat:	4
Carbohydrates:	15 g
Protein:	1 g
Cholesterol:	0 mg
Sodium:	50 mg

2 FRESH FRUIT & MORE

Fruit is wonderful when served warm from the rotisserie and it is especially good when sweetened with a bit of spice. The recipes that follow are good accompaniments to pork, ham or poultry. Also, because fruits are naturally sweet, George enjoys warming them in the rotisserie without using any spices or seasonings. Simply heat any firm fruit in the adjustable basket of the rotisserie for an outstanding meal accompaniment!

Cinnamon Papaya

Papaya releases all it's flavor when gently warmed.

2	ripe papaya
1/4 c.	lowfat margarine, softened
1/2 t.	cinnamon
2 T.	honey

NUTRITIONAL ANALYSIS	
Calories:	144
Total fat:	6 g
Saturated fat:	1 g
% calories fat:	34
Carbohydrates:	25 g
Protein:	1 g
Cholesterol:	0 mg
Sodium:	81 mg

Cut the papaya into halves, scoop out the seeds and pat dry. In a small bowl, combine the margarine, cinnamon and honey and brush over the papaya evenly. Place the papaya in the adjustable basket as directed in the Owner's Manual. Set the Timer for 15 minutes and cook at 425°F. When cooked, brush any remaining cinnamon mixture over the papaya. Serves 4.

Sweet Cinnamon Pears

This is a treat whenever firm pears are in season.

4	ripe, firm pears (Bosc or Anjou)
1/4 c.	sugar
1/2 c.	unsweetened apple juice
1/2 t.	ground cinnamon

NUTRITIONAL ANALYSIS	
Calories:	187
Total fat:	<1 g
Saturated fat:	<1 g
% calories fat:	4
Carbohydrates:	48 g
Protein:	1 g
Cholesterol:	0 mg
Sodium:	2 mg

Combine the sugar, juice and ground cinnamon in a small saucepan and heat. Boil for five minutes, until the sugar is dissolved and flavors have blended. Cool. Cut the pears in half and place in the adjustable basket as directed in the Owner's Manual. Brush with the glaze. Set the Timer for 15 minutes and cook at 425°F. Pour a small amount of the glaze onto 4 individual plates and arrange two pear halves on top of each pool of sauce. Serves 4.

Pineapple & Honey Rotisserie

An unusual treat for a very special meal.

1	medium pineapple
1 t.	water
¼ c.	honey

NUTRITIONAL ANALYSIS

Calories:	61
Total fat:	<1 g
Saturated fat:	<1 g
% calories fat:	3
Carbohydrates:	16 g
Protein:	<1 g
Cholesterol:	0 mg
Sodium:	1 mg

With a sharp knife, cut the leaves off the top of the pineapple. Carefully cut the peel off the pineapple, leaving the fruit and core. Center the pineapple on the rotisserie bar as directed in the Owner's Manual. In a small saucepan, heat the honey and water until warm. Place the pineapple in the rotisserie and brush entirely with the honey. Set the Timer for 15 minutes and cook at 425°F. When the pineapple is cooked, remove it from the rotisserie bar, cut in half and core. Slice ½-inch thick pieces. Place the slices on a serving platter and drizzle remaining honey on top. Serves 8.

Sugared Rotisserie Peaches

Cook ham steaks and add these peaches for a satisfying dinner.

4	firm peaches, peeled, pitted and cut in half
8	whole cloves
1 t.	ground cinnamon
1 c.	sugar

NUTRITIONAL ANALYSIS	
Calories:	116
Total fat:	<1 g
Saturated fat:	<1 g
% calories fat:	1
Carbohydrates:	30 g
Protein:	<1 g
Cholesterol:	0 mg
Sodium:	<1 mg

Push 1 clove into each peach half. In a small bowl, combine the cinnamon and the sugar. Roll each peach half in the cinnamon mixture. Place the peaches in the adjustable basket as directed in the Owner's Manual. Set the Timer for 15 minutes and cook at 425°F. Remove the cloves before eating. Serves 8.

Grilled Apple Slices

Tangy and sweet flavors combine to partner with the apples.

3	large, firm apples
3 T.	orange juice
1 t.	ground cinnamon
1/2 c.	sugar

NUTRITIONAL ANALYSIS	
Calories:	132
Total fat:	<1 g
Saturated fat:	<1 g
% calories fat:	3
Carbohydrates:	34 g
Protein:	<1 g
Cholesterol:	0 mg
Sodium:	0 mg

Core the apples and slice into rounds 1-inch thick. Place the apple slices in a shallow pan and drizzle the orange juice over the slices, turning to coat. Mix together the cinnamon and sugar and sprinkle over each slice. Turn the slices and sprinkle again. Place the slices in the adjustable basket as directed in the Owner's Manual. Set the Timer for 15 minutes and cook at 425°F. Serves 6.

3 SALADS: AROUND THE WORLD AND BACK HOME AGAIN

Salads have long been established as part of a healthy eating plan, but only within the last few years have salads begun to taste so wonderfully good that we now also enjoy them as main dishes. What piqued our appetites for salad? The answer lies in the introduction of foods and flavor combinations from around the world—Thai Sirloin Salad, Chicken Nacho Salad, Italian Minestrone Salad and Oriental Chicken Salad, just to name a few. Enjoy the creative salad recipes that follow and know that you're treating yourself to good health, as well!

Grilled Chicken Caesar Salad

Prepare the chicken ahead of time for a fast and easy entrée.

2	boneless, skinless chicken breast halves
2 T.	minced garlic
2 T.	Worcestershire sauce
1 T.	chili powder
1/2 t.	pepper
1/2 c.	lowfat buttermilk
1/4 c.	lowfat grated Parmesan cheese
1 T.	lemon juice
1 t.	anchovy paste (optional)
	pepper to taste
1 T.	minced garlic
12 c.	romaine lettuce, cleaned and torn
2 c.	cherry tomatoes
3/4 c.	lowfat toasted croutons

NUTRITIONAL ANALYSIS

Calories:	259
Total fat:	5 g
Saturated fat:	1 g
% calories fat:	16
Carbohydrates:	19 g
Protein:	36 g
Cholesterol:	82 mg
Sodium:	867 mg

Place the chicken breasts in a shallow glass pan. In a small bowl, combine the garlic, Worcestershire sauce, chili powder, and pepper. Brush the breasts with the sauce and refrigerate for 20 minutes. Place the chicken breasts in the adjustable basket of the rotisserie as directed by the Owner's Manual. Set the Timer for 15–20 minutes and cook at 425°F. When the chicken is done, cool and slice. Combine the buttermilk, cheese, juice, anchovy paste and pepper. Blend thoroughly. In a large salad bowl, place the lettuce, tomatoes and croutons. Coat with the dressing and toss. Divide the salad among four plates and place the chicken strips on top. Sprinkle additional Parmesan cheese on top, if desired. Serves 4.

Mexicali Chicken Salad

Colorful and flavorful, too!

2	boneless, skinless chicken breast halves
8 oz.	large pasta noodle shells, uncooked
1	4 oz. can chopped green chiles, drained
1/4 c.	sliced ripe olives
1 c.	chopped tomatoes
2 T.	chopped fresh cilantro
1/4 c.	chopped green onion
1/4 c.	chopped green pepper
1 T.	lemon juice
2 t.	olive oil
1 t.	pepper
1 T.	minced garlic

NUTRITIONAL ANALYSIS

Calories:	355
Total fat:	7 g
Saturated fat:	1 g
% calories fat:	19
Carbohydrates:	39 g
Protein:	34 g
Cholesterol:	73 mg
Sodium:	242 mg

Place the chicken breasts in the adjustable basket of the rotisserie as directed in the Owner's Manual. Set the Timer for 15–20 minutes and cook at 425°F. Cool and shred the chicken into small pieces. In a large pot, bring 3 quarts of water to boil. Add the pasta shells and cook approximately 12 minutes, or until tender. Drain and keep warm. Combine the chicken, chiles, olives, tomatoes, cilantro, green onion, green pepper, juice, oil, pepper and garlic in a large bowl. Toss gently to blend flavors. Add the pasta and toss again. Serve warm or cold. Serves 4.

German Potato Salad

This new, lowfat version offers wonderful flavor.
Serve with Oktoberfest Rotisserie Chicken (p. 95).

9	medium red potatoes
6	turkey bacon slices
1	hard-cooked egg, peeled and chopped
1	chopped onion

Dressing:

3 T.	flour
$1/2$ c.	water
$1/2$ c.	sugar
$1/2$ c.	cider vinegar
1 c.	fat-free sour cream

NUTRITIONAL ANALYSIS

Calories: 363
Total fat: 4 g
Saturated fat: 1 g
% calories fat: 9
Carbohydrates: 73 g
Protein: 10 g
Cholesterol: 51 mg
Sodium: 238 mg

Cook potatoes until tender. Drain and cool. Cut potatoes into ¼-inch thick slices. Cook the bacon and crumble into small pieces. In a large bowl, combine potatoes, bacon, egg and onion. In a small saucepan, mix flour, water, sugar and vinegar. Heat and stir until the dressing is smooth and thick. Remove from the heat and add the sour cream. Mix well. Pour the dressing over the potato mixture and toss gently. Serve warm. Serves 6.

Cajun Turkey Salad

Use up leftover turkey in a flash!

3	boneless, skinless turkey breast pieces (about 10 oz.)
2 T.	spicy Cajun seasoning
1 T.	sugar
3 T.	cider vinegar
1/2 t.	salt
1/4 t.	pepper
1/4 c.	lemon juice
3 T.	Dijon mustard
3 T.	water
1 T.	honey
2 c.	chopped tomatoes
1	medium green pepper
1	medium red pepper
1/2 c.	chopped red onion
8 c.	torn dark-green lettuce

NUTRITIONAL ANALYSIS

Calories:	194
Total fat:	2 g
Saturated fat:	<1 g
% calories fat:	10
Carbohydrates:	24 g
Protein:	22 g
Cholesterol:	96 mg
Sodium:	386 mg

Place the turkey breast in the adjustable basket of the rotisserie as directed in the Owner's Manual. Set the Timer for 15 minutes and cook at 425°F. Cool and shred the turkey into small pieces. In a large bowl, toss the turkey with the Cajun seasoning. In a small bowl, combine the sugar, vinegar, salt, pepper, juice, mustard, water and honey to make the dressing. Whisk the ingredients together and chill. Add the tomatoes, peppers, onion and lettuce to the turkey and mix well. Pour the dressing over the top of all. Toss again and chill for 10 minutes. Serves 4.

Oriental Chicken Salad

The piquant flavor of fresh ginger spikes this salad nicely.

2	boneless, skinless chicken breast halves
1/2 c.	nonfat chicken broth
2 T.	sliced fresh ginger
1 T.	minced garlic
1/4 c.	rice wine vinegar
1 T.	vegetable oil
2 T.	grated fresh ginger
2 T.	soy sauce
1 T.	minced garlic
1/4 t.	red pepper flakes
1/2	head cabbage, thinly sliced
1/2 c.	bean sprouts, washed and drained
1	chopped red pepper
1/4 c.	chopped green onion

NUTRITIONAL ANALYSIS

Calories: 106
Total fat: 4 g
Saturated fat: <1 g
% calories fat: 30
Carbohydrates: 8 g
Protein: 11 g
Cholesterol: 24 mg
Sodium: 394 mg

Place the chicken in the adjustable basket of the rotisserie as directed in the Owner's Manual. Set the Timer for 15 minutes and cook at 425°F. Cool and shred the chicken. In a medium bowl, mix the chicken with the broth, sliced ginger and garlic. Chill for 2 hours to allow flavors to blend. In a small bowl, whisk together the vinegar, oil, grated ginger, soy sauce, garlic and red pepper. Chill. In a large salad bowl mix together the cabbage, bean sprouts, red pepper and green onion. Add the drained chicken and the chilled dressing. Mix well. Serves 6.

Crunchy Cucumber Salad

A cool, refreshing salad that goes well with Tandoori Rotisserie Beef (p. 62).

2 c.	cold water
2 c.	cider vinegar
$1/2$ c.	sugar
1 t.	salt
4	large cucumbers, peeled and sliced $1/4$-inch thick
1	small red onion, thinly sliced
2 T.	chopped fresh parsley

NUTRITIONAL ANALYSIS

Calories:	82
Total fat:	<1 g
Saturated fat:	<1 g
% calories fat:	2
Carbohydrates:	21 g
Protein:	1 g
Cholesterol:	0 mg
Sodium:	297 mg

In a medium bowl combine the water, vinegar, sugar and salt. Stir well to dissolve the sugar. Add the cucumbers, onion and parsley. Refrigerate 4–8 hours. Drain and serve. Serves 8.

Sirloin & Broccoli Linguine

A hearty, full-meal salad.

1	12 oz. beef sirloin steak
8 oz.	linguine noodles, cooked and drained
1	chopped tomato
1	chopped red pepper
1 c.	broccoli cuts, cooked and cooled
1	chopped carrot
1	chopped red onion

Dressing:

1/2 c.	lowfat mayonnaise
1/2 t.	dill
2 T.	blue cheese
1 T.	minced garlic
1 T.	cider vinegar
1 t.	lemon juice

NUTRITIONAL ANALYSIS	
Calories:	357
Total fat:	7 g
Saturated fat:	3 g
% calories fat:	20
Carbohydrates:	26 g
Protein:	40 g
Cholesterol:	79 mg
Sodium:	417 mg

Place the sirloin steak in the adjustable basket of the rotisserie as directed in the Owner's Manual. Set the Timer for 20 minutes and cook at 450°F. Cool and slice thinly. In a large bowl, combine the steak, noodles, tomato, red pepper, broccoli, carrot and onion. Make the dressing by mixing together the mayonnaise, dill, blue cheese, garlic, vinegar and lemon juice. Whisk together and pour over the beef and pasta salad. Serves 4.

Favorite Bean Salad

This salad is a classic in a new lower-fat version and it's a perfect accompaniment to Deli Rotisserie Chicken (p. 94).

1	16 oz. can black beans, drained
1	16 oz. can kidney beans, drained
1	10 oz. can whole-kernel corn, drained
1/4 c.	chopped green onion
1 T.	finely chopped parsley

Dressing:

2 T.	cider vinegar
2 T.	lemon juice
2 T.	olive oil
1/2 t.	pepper

NUTRITIONAL ANALYSIS

Calories: 172
Total fat: 4 g
Saturated fat: <1 g
% calories fat: 22
Carbohydrates: 27 g
Protein: 8 g
Cholesterol: 0 mg
Sodium: 251 mg

In a large salad bowl, combine the beans, corn, green onions, and parsley. In a small bowl, combine the vinegar, juice, oil and pepper. Mix well and toss with the beans and vegetables. Cover tightly and refrigerate 6–12 hours. Serves 8.

Herbed Chicken & Crouton Salad

Both salad and bread in one unusual dish!

1	loaf Italian bread, unsliced
2	boneless, skinless chicken breast halves
2 c.	chopped tomatoes
1/2 c.	chopped green pepper
1/2 c.	chopped red onion
1/2 c.	chopped celery

Dressing:

1 t.	dried Italian seasoning
2 T.	olive oil
1/4 c.	water
2 T.	cider vinegar
1 T.	minced garlic
1 t.	salt
1/2 t.	pepper

NUTRITIONAL ANALYSIS	
Calories:	439
Total fat:	10 g
Saturated fat:	2 g
% calories fat:	21
Carbohydrates:	62 g
Protein:	24 g
Cholesterol:	36 mg
Sodium:	1480 mg

Remove the crusts from the bread and cut into ½-inch cubes. Measure 4 cups and save the remainder for another use. Place the bread cubes on the baking sheet of the rotisserie. Set the Timer for 10 minutes and bake at 425°F. Cool. Place the chicken in the adjustable basket of the rotisserie as directed in the Owner's Manual. Set the Timer for 15 minutes and cook at 425°F. Cool and cut the chicken into cubes. In a large salad bowl, combine the bread cubes, chicken, tomatoes, green pepper, onion and celery. In a small bowl, combine the Italian seasoning, oil, water, vinegar, garlic, salt and pepper. Mix well to blend the flavors and pour the dressing over the salad. Serves 4.

Crisp & Spicy BBQ Coleslaw

Serve with Southern Party Pork Roast (p. 75), for an outstanding meal!

1/2 c.	lemon juice
1/2 c.	sugar
2 T.	vegetable oil
1 t.	salt
1/2 t.	dry mustard
5 c.	finely shredded cabbage
1/2 c.	chopped green pepper
1/2 c.	sliced green onion
1/2 c.	shredded carrot

NUTRITIONAL ANALYSIS

Calories:	82
Total fat:	3 g
Saturated fat:	<1 g
% calories fat:	30
Carbohydrates:	14 g
Protein:	<1 g
Cholesterol:	0 mg
Sodium:	242 mg

In a small saucepan, combine the juice, sugar, oil, salt and dry mustard. Heat to boiling and stir for 2 minutes. Place the cabbage, green pepper, onion and carrot in a large salad bowl and pour the dressing over all. Cover tightly with plastic wrap and refrigerate 4–12 hours. Toss again just before serving. Serves 10.

Pepper & Cilantro Chicken Salad

This is a refreshing and colorful salad.

2	boneless, skinless chicken breast halves
1	chopped red pepper
1	chopped red onion
1 t.	jalapeno pepper, seeded and chopped
2 c.	chopped tomatoes
8 c.	torn green leaf lettuce

Dressing:

1 T.	olive oil
1/2 c.	lemon juice
2 t.	chili powder
1 T.	minced garlic
1 t.	ground cumin
1/2 t.	pepper

NUTRITIONAL ANALYSIS

Calories: 112
Total fat: 4 g
Saturated fat: <1 g
% calories fat: 29
Carbohydrates: 10 g
Protein: 11 g
Cholesterol: 24 mg
Sodium: 42 mg

Place the chicken in the adjustable basket of the rotisserie as directed by the Owner's Manual. Set the Timer for 15 minutes and cook at 425°F. Cool and shred into small pieces. Combine the chicken, red pepper, onion, jalapeno pepper, tomatoes and lettuce in a large salad bowl. Combine the remaining ingredients and whisk smoothly. Pour the dressing over the salad and chill slightly. Serves 6.

Italian Minestrone Salad

Just as the name implies, this spicy salad includes the ingredients for Minestrone. Serve with Herbed Veal Rotisserie Roast (p. 73), for a special occasion.

4 oz.	vermicelli pasta, cooked and drained
1 c.	small white beans, cooked
1/4 c.	chopped green onion
1	zucchini, cut into matchstick pieces
1	carrot, cut into thin strips
2 c.	canned green beans
2 c.	chopped tomatoes

Dressing:

1/4 c.	chopped fresh basil
2 T.	chopped fresh parsley
2 T.	balsamic vinegar
2 T.	lime juice
1 t.	olive oil
2 T.	water
1/2 t.	pepper

NUTRITIONAL ANALYSIS

Calories:	177
Total fat:	2 g
Saturated fat:	<1 g
% calories fat:	10
Carbohydrates:	33 g
Protein:	8 g
Cholesterol:	0 mg
Sodium:	361 mg

In a large salad bowl, combine the pasta, white beans, green onions, zucchini, carrot, green beans and tomatoes. In a small bowl, mix together the basil, parsley, vinegar, lime juice, oil, water and pepper. Whisk together to blend well. Pour the dressing over the salad and mix well. Serves 4.

Thai Steak Salad

This is a great luncheon salad with a beautiful presentation.

1	8 oz.	beef sirloin steak
2 t.		soy sauce
2 T.		lime juice
2 T.		fish sauce
1 T.		minced garlic
1/2 t.		red chile pepper flakes
1		sliced red onion
1		sliced and peeled cucumber
1		sliced red pepper
8 c.		torn Romaine lettuce leaves

NUTRITIONAL ANALYSIS

Calories:	159
Total fat:	3 g
Saturated fat:	2 g
% calories fat:	17
Carbohydrates:	10 g
Protein:	21 g
Cholesterol:	50 mg
Sodium:	915 mg

Place the sirloin into the adjustable basket of the rotisserie as directed in the Owner's Manual. Set the Timer for 15 minutes and cook at 450°F. Cool and slice thinly. In a small bowl, combine the soy sauce, lime juice, fish sauce, garlic and chile pepper flakes. Mix well. In a large salad bowl, combine the steak, onion, cucumber, red pepper and lettuce. Pour the dressing over the steak and vegetables and toss. Serves 4.

Cancun Chicken Salad

This spicy chicken salad is especially good when chilled.

2	8-inch flour tortillas
2	boneless, skinless chicken breast halves
8 c.	shredded lettuce
1	sliced red onion
1	sliced red pepper
1 T.	chopped fresh parsley
2 T.	chopped fresh cilantro

Dressing:

1 T.	wine vinegar
1/4 t.	cumin
1 t.	lime juice
1/2 t.	sugar
1 T.	minced garlic
1/2 t.	chili powder
1/2 t.	pepper

NUTRITIONAL ANALYSIS	
Calories:	196
Total fat:	4 g
Saturated fat:	<1 g
% calories fat:	17
Carbohydrates:	23 g
Protein:	18 g
Cholesterol:	36 mg
Sodium:	163 mg

Place the tortillas on the rotisserie baking sheet. Cut each into long, thin slices. Set the Timer for 15 minutes and bake at 425°F. Cool and set aside. Place the chicken in the adjustable basket of the rotisserie as directed in the Owner's Manual. Set the Timer for 15 minutes and cook at 425°F. Cool and shred into small pieces. In a large bowl combine the chicken, lettuce, onion, red pepper, parsley and cilantro. In a small bowl, mix the vinegar, cumin, lime juice, sugar, garlic, chili powder and pepper. Pour the dressing over the chicken salad and mix well. Garnish with the crisp tortilla strips. Serves 4.

GRAINS & PASTA: ENTERTAINING SIDE DISHES

Grains and pasta are important sources of carbohydrates and, when served with fresh and entertaining flavors, they can add texture and taste to any meal. Although the calories may be high occasionally, you can compensate by making your portions a bit smaller. Or, you may want to use any of these recipes as your entrée to enjoy with a small salad.

Mediterranean Rice Pilaf

Try serving this with Mint & Rosemary Lamb Kebabs (p. 88).

1 c.	chopped onion
2 T.	minced garlic
1 t.	olive oil
1 c.	uncooked long-grain white rice
2 c.	fat-free chicken broth
2 c.	chopped tomato
8	Kalamata olives, pitted and sliced
1/4 c.	chopped green onion
1 c.	shredded lowfat Mozzarella cheese

NUTRITIONAL ANALYSIS

Calories:	215
Total fat:	4 g
Saturated fat:	1 g
% calories fat:	16
Carbohydrates:	34 g
Protein:	11 g
Cholesterol:	4 mg
Sodium:	246 mg

In a large saucepan, sauté the onion and garlic in the olive oil until tender. Add the rice and broth and bring to a boil. Reduce the heat, cover and simmer for 20 minutes. Stir in the tomato, olives and green onions. Divide the pilaf into six portions and top each with Mozzarella cheese. Serves 6.

Broccoli Risotto

This Italian risotto is very moist and rich-tasting. For a special treat, serve with Siccilian Herb Rotisserie Chicken (p. 97).

1	10 $^3/_4$ oz. can 99% fat-free cream of mushroom soup
2 T.	finely chopped onion
$^1/_2$ c.	fat-free sour cream
1	2 oz. pkg. dry ranch dressing mix
1	14 oz. can fat-free chicken broth
2 c.	uncooked instant rice
$1^1/_2$ c.	chopped fresh broccoli
1	6 oz. can sliced mushrooms, drained
$^1/_2$ t.	pepper
$^1/_2$ c.	grated fat-free cheddar cheese

NUTRITIONAL ANALYSIS

Calories:	165
Total fat:	<1 g
Saturated fat:	<1 g
% calories fat:	4
Carbohydrates:	28 g
Protein:	8 g
Cholesterol:	3 mg
Sodium:	749 mg

In a large bowl, combine the soup, onion, sour cream, dressing mix and chicken broth. Mix well until smooth. Add the rice, broccoli, mushrooms, pepper and cheese and combine thoroughly. Spray a 9" x 13" glass casserole pan with non-stick cooking spray and pour the risotto into it. Cover with aluminum foil. Place the wire rack on the lower shelf position of the rotisserie and put the casserole on the wire rack. Set the Timer for 40 minutes and bake at 425°F. Serves 8.

Sun-Dried Tomato Rigatoni

Bold flavors and cheese make this a memorable pasta dish.

1 t.	olive oil
1 c.	sliced fresh mushrooms
1 lb.	rigatoni, cooked and drained
1	15 oz. nonfat ricotta cheese
1/4 c.	oil-packed sun-dried tomatoes, drained and dried with paper towels
1 c.	sliced black olives
1 T.	chopped fresh parsley
1 c.	shredded lowfat mozzarella cheese

NUTRITIONAL ANALYSIS

Calories:	174
Total fat:	4 g
Saturated fat:	1 g
% calories fat:	21
Carbohydrates:	22 g
Protein:	13 g
Cholesterol:	3 mg
Sodium:	307 mg

Heat the olive oil in a small pan and add the mushrooms. Cook until the mushrooms are tender. In a large bowl, combine the mushrooms, rigatoni, ricotta cheese, sun-dried tomatoes, olives, parsley and ½ cup of the cheese. Mix well and pour into a 9" x 13" casserole dish. Top with the remaining cheese and cover with aluminum foil. Place the wire rack in the lower shelf position of the rotisserie. Put the casserole on top of the wire rack. Set the Timer for 30–35 minutes and bake at 425°F. Serves 8.

Cheese & Bacon Ziti

Rich and spicy flavors partner together in this pasta dish. Serve with Italian Rotisserie Chicken Breasts (p. 108), for an easy weeknight meal.

8	slices turkey bacon
8 oz.	ziti pasta, cooked and drained
2 T.	minced garlic
2 c.	shredded lowfat mozzarella cheese
1/4 c.	grated lowfat Parmesan cheese
1/4 t.	chili powder
3 T.	chopped fresh parsley

NUTRITIONAL ANALYSIS	
Calories:	191
Total fat:	5 g
Saturated fat:	2 g
% calories fat:	24
Carbohydrates:	21 g
Protein:	15 g
Cholesterol:	20 mg
Sodium:	394 mg

Cook the bacon until crisp and break into small pieces. In a large serving bowl, combine the bacon, ziti, garlic, mozzarella and Parmesan cheese. Add the chili powder and the parsley and toss well. Serve warm. Serves 8.

Herb & Garlic Linguine

The mild flavors of this linguine accompany Grandma's Peppered Beef Roast (p. 59), very well.

$1/4$ c.	lowfat margarine
1 T.	minced garlic
14 oz.	linguine, cooked
$1/4$ c.	chopped fresh parsley
$1/2$ t.	dried oregano
$1/2$ c.	grated lowfat Parmesan cheese

NUTRITIONAL ANALYSIS

Calories:	212
Total fat:	7 g
Saturated fat:	1 g
% calories fat:	30
Carbohydrates:	26 g
Protein:	10 g
Cholesterol:	43 mg
Sodium:	317 mg

In a medium saucepan, cook the garlic in the margarine until tender. Add the linguine, parsley, oregano and cheese. Mix well to combine the flavors and serve immediately. Serves 4.

Zucchini & Eggplant Pasta

This is a good way to use your fresh, home-grown vegetables.

1	medium zucchini, cut into cubes
1	small eggplant, cut into cubes
1 T.	minced garlic
1 T.	olive oil
4 oz.	bow tie pasta, cooked and drained
1 c.	chopped red onion
1 t.	dried basil
½ t.	salt
½ t.	pepper
1 c.	lowfat shredded mozzarella cheese

NUTRITIONAL ANALYSIS

Calories:	257
Total fat:	6 g
Saturated fat:	2 g
% calories fat:	21
Carbohydrates:	38 g
Protein:	14 g
Cholesterol:	6 mg
Sodium:	447mg

Place the zucchini and eggplant in the roasted veggie/air bake basket as directed in the Owner's Manual. Set the Timer for 30–35 minutes and bake at 425°F. In a large pan, heat the garlic in the oil until tender. Add the pasta, zucchini, eggplant, onion, basil, salt and pepper. Heat just until warm and add the cheese. Toss and serve. Serves 4.

5 BREADS & MUFFINS: GOOD-FOR-YOU AND OH, SO GOOD

Breads and muffins don't have to be high-fat and loaded with calories to taste good. These recipes offer a variety of breads with pleasing textures and deliciously rich flavors. Whether you are cooking for guests or simply looking for a nice addition to your meal, you can select any of these recipes to add a simple bit of pleasure to the day.

Soft Italian Focaccia Breadsticks

Warm-from-the-oven goodness!

1 pkg.	active dry yeast
1 c.	warm water (105°–115°F)
2 t.	sugar
1 t.	salt
3 T.	lowfat margarine, softened
2¾ c.	all-purpose flour
1 T.	lowfat margarine
1 t.	dried Italian seasoning
1 t.	black pepper
½ t.	salt
½ t.	dried oregano
	non-stick cooking spray

NUTRITIONAL ANALYSIS

Calories: 50
Total fat: <1 g
Saturated fat: <1 g
% calories fat: 17
Carbohydrates: 9 g
Protein: 1 g
Cholesterol: 0 mg
Sodium: 138 mg

Dissolve yeast in the warm water in a large bowl and add the sugar, salt and margarine. Stir in the flour, mixing to make a smooth dough. Turn the dough onto a lightly floured surface and knead until smooth, about 5 minutes. Shape into a ball and let rest 10 minutes. Lightly coat the rotisserie baking sheet with cooking spray and press the dough to fit the sheet. Brush with the margarine and sprinkle with the Italian seasoning, black pepper, salt and dried oregano. Place the baking sheet in the rotisserie as directed in the Owner's Manual. Set the Timer for 20 minutes and bake at 450°F. Bread will be lightly browned on the bottom. Remove the baking sheet from the rotisserie. Cool slightly and cut the bread in half lengthwise. Cut each half into 14 sticks about 1-inch wide. Makes 28 breadsticks.

Grandma's Homemade Corn Bread

Great with all rotisserie meats!

1$\frac{1}{2}$ c.	yellow cornmeal
$\frac{1}{2}$ c.	white flour
1 T.	baking powder
2	egg whites
1 c.	nonfat milk
1	14$\frac{3}{4}$ oz. can creamed corn
$\frac{1}{4}$ c.	chopped onion
1	4 oz. can chopped green chiles, drained
	non-stick cooking spray

NUTRITIONAL ANALYSIS

Calories:	138
Total fat:	<1 g
Saturated fat:	<1 g
% calories fat:	6
Carbohydrates:	29 g
Protein:	5 g
Cholesterol:	0 mg
Sodium:	439 mg

Mix the cornmeal, flour and baking powder in a medium bowl. Add the egg whites, milk, corn, onion and chiles and stir to blend well. Spray a 9" x 13" glass pan lightly with non-stick cooking spray and pour the cornbread into it. Place the wire rack on the lower shelf of the rotisserie and put the cornbread on the rack. Set the Timer for 25–30 minutes and cook at 425°F until golden brown. Serves 10.

Herbed Polenta

This quick and easy polenta goes well with poultry.

1	24 oz. roll prepared polenta
1 T.	dried Italian seasoning
½ t.	salt
½ t.	pepper
1 T.	chopped fresh parsley
	non-stick, butter-flavored spray

Slice the polenta into ½-inch thick slices. Coat the rotisserie baking sheet with the buttered-flavored spray and place the slices on the sheet. Lightly coat the top of each slice with the spray. Mix together the Italian seasoning, salt, pepper and parsley and sprinkle of top of each slice. Set the Timer for 15–20 minutes and cook at 425°F. Serve immediately. Serves 6.

Onion Dill Sandwich Buns

Slice and toast for excellent luncheon sandwiches.

1	pkg. active dry yeast
1 c.	warm water, 105–115°F
3 T.	sugar
2 T.	snipped fresh dill
1 T.	vegetable oil
2 t.	salt
1/2 c.	finely minced onion
3 1/2 c.	bread flour
	non-stick cooking spray

NUTRITIONAL ANALYSIS

Calories:	190
Total fat:	2 g
Saturated fat:	<1 g
% calories fat:	9
Carbohydrates:	37 g
Protein:	6 g
Cholesterol:	0 mg
Sodium:	467 mg

In a small bowl, combine the yeast and the water. Stir to dissolve the yeast completely. In a large mixing bowl, place the yeast mixture, sugar, dill, oil, salt, onion and bread flour. Mix until the ingredients are blended and the dough is smooth. Turn onto a lightly floured board and knead for 5 minutes. Let the dough rest for 10 minutes. Lightly spray a large bowl with non-stick cooking spray and place the dough in it to rise, about 2 hours. Punch down. Lightly coat the rotisserie baking sheet with non-stick cooking spray. Divide the dough and shape into 10 bun-shaped rounds on the baking sheet. Cover and rise again for approximately 1 hour. Set the Timer for 30–35 minutes and bake at 425°F. Makes 10 buns.

Favorite Banana Muffins

A classic taste in a new lower-fat version.

3/4 c.	sugar
1/2 c.	lowfat margarine
1	egg
3	egg whites
1 1/4 c.	ripe banana, mashed
1/4 c.	water
1 3/4 c.	flour
2 t.	baking soda
1/2 t.	salt
1/2 t.	cinnamon
1/4 t.	baking powder
	non-stick cooking spray

NUTRITIONAL ANALYSIS	
Calories:	185
Total fat:	4 g
Saturated fat:	<1 g
% calories fat:	21
Carbohydrates:	33 g
Protein:	4 g
Cholesterol:	16 mg
Sodium:	399 mg

In a medium bowl, beat the sugar and margarine until light. Beat in the egg, egg whites, banana and water until well-blended. Mix in the flour, baking soda, salt, cinnamon and baking powder and stir just until all ingredients are moistened. Lightly coat a 12-cup muffin pan with with the spray (or line with paper liners) and fill each cup 1/2 full with the batter. Put the wire rack on the lower shelf position of the rotisserie and place the muffin pan on the rack. Set the Timer for 15 minutes and bake at 425°F. Makes 12 muffins.

Blueberry Bran Muffins

A wholesome morning treat.

1 c.	buttermilk
2	egg whites
2 T.	vegetable oil
1¼ c.	whole wheat flour
1 c.	oat bran
½ c.	brown sugar, packed
3 t.	baking powder
¼ t.	baking soda
¼ t.	salt
¼ t.	nutmeg
¼ t.	cinnamon
1 c.	blueberries
	non-stick cooking spray

NUTRITIONAL ANALYSIS

Calories:	135
Total fat:	3 g
Saturated fat:	<1 g
% calories fat:	19
Carbohydrates:	26 g
Protein:	4 g
Cholesterol:	<1 mg
Sodium:	241 mg

In a large bowl, mix the buttermilk, egg whites and oil. Blend in the flour, bran, sugar, baking powder, baking soda, salt, nutmeg and cinnamon. Stir just until all ingredients are moistened. Fold in the blueberries. Lightly coat a 12-cup muffin pan with with the spray (or line with paper liners) and fill each cup ½ full with the batter. Put the wire rack on the lower shelf of the rotisserie and place the muffin pan on the rack. Set the Timer for 15 minutes and bake at 425°F. Makes 12 muffins.

6 DESSERTS: LUSCIOUS & LOWFAT

Desserts often complete our meals in the most satisfying way, but they are traditionally forbidden because of the high fat associated with them. The low-fat recipes in this section have been specifically created by Connie to give you dessert choices that are tempting and tasty while knocking out that unhealthy fat. So, enjoy desserts in moderation, knowing that a bit of sweet indulgence can also be a healthy choice.

Homemade Chocolate Chip Cookies

"Comfort food" at it's best!

1 c.	unsweetened applesauce
1/2 c.	sugar
1 c.	packed brown sugar
1 t.	vanilla
1/2 c.	nonfat egg product
2 3/4 c.	flour
1 t.	baking soda
1 t.	salt
1	12 oz. pkg. chocolate chips

NUTRITIONAL ANALYSIS	
Calories:	146
Total fat:	4 g
Saturated fat:	2 g
% calories fat:	21
Carbohydrates:	28 g
Protein:	2 g
Cholesterol:	0 mg
Sodium:	131 mg

In a large mixing bowl, combine the applesauce, sugar, brown sugar, vanilla and egg product. Beat well. In a small bowl, combine the flour, baking soda and salt. Add to the batter and blend again. Fold in the chocolate chips. Drop the batter by rounded teapoons on the ungreased rotisserie baking sheet, about 1 inch apart. Set the Timer for 10–12 minutes and cook at 400°F. Repeat with the remaining cookie dough. Makes 3 dozen cookies, 2 cookies per serving.

Boysenberry Cobbler

Great with fresh boysenberries!

1¹/₂ c.	lowfat biscuit mix
1 c.	nonfat milk
¹/₄ c.	sugar
4 c.	fresh boysenberries (or other seasonal fruit)
¹/₂ c.	sugar
1 t.	lemon juice
1 T.	lowfat margarine
	non-stick cooking spray

NUTRITIONAL ANALYSIS	
Calories:	109
Total fat:	<1 g
Saturated fat:	<1 g
% calories fat:	5
Carbohydrates:	25 g
Protein:	25 g
Cholesterol:	2 mg
Sodium:	183 mg

In a medium bowl, combine the biscuit mix, milk and sugar. Stir until blended. Lightly coat a 9" x 13" baking dish with the cooking spray and spoon two-thirds of the biscuit batter into the bottom, smoothing to make an even layer. In a medium bowl, combine the boysenberries, sugar, lemon juice and margarine and pour over the batter. Dot the remaining batter on the top. Sprinkle a bit of sugar and cinnamon over the top, if desired. Place the wire rack on the lower shelf position of the rotisserie and put the cobbler on the rack. Set the Timer for 25–30 minutes and bake at 425°F. Serves 16.

Chocolate Cream Pie

A family favorite for summertime.

12	graham cracker squares, ground
1/4 c.	sugar
1/4 c.	lowfat margarine
1	3 oz. pkg. instant, fat-free, chocolate fudge pudding and pie filling
2 c.	nonfat milk
1	8 oz. carton fat-free whipped topping
	non-stick cooking spray

NUTRITIONAL ANALYSIS

Calories:	280
Total fat:	4 g
Saturated fat:	<1 g
% calories fat:	18
Carbohydrates:	38 g
Protein:	6 g
Cholesterol:	2 mg
Sodium:	309 mg

Combine the graham cracker crumbs with the sugar and lowfat margarine. Press into the bottom of a 9-inch pie pan. Place the wire rack on the lower shelf position of the rotisserie and put the pie pan on top of the rack. Set the Timer for 12 minutes and bake at 425°F. The crust will be lightly browned. Cool the crust while preparing the chocolate cream. In a medium bowl, combine the pudding mix with the milk and let the pudding chill in the refrigerator for 5 minutes. Fold the whipped topping into the chilled pudding and pour into the pie plate. Freeze 8 hours or until solid. Serves 6.

Gingerbread

Dollop with nonfat whipped topping for a guilt-free treat!

1/4 c.	applesauce
1/4 c.	fat-free sour cream
2	egg whites
1 c.	molasses
2 1/2 c.	flour
2 t.	baking soda
1/2 t.	salt
1 t.	cinnamon
1 t.	ginger
1 t.	nutmeg
1 t.	ground cloves
1 c.	hot water
1/2 c.	sugar
1 c.	powdered sugar
1/4 c.	lemon juice
	non-stick cooking spray

NUTRITIONAL ANALYSIS

Calories:	195
Total fat:	<1 g
Saturated fat:	0 g
% calories fat:	2
Carbohydrates:	45 g
Protein:	3 g
Cholesterol:	<1 mg
Sodium:	255 mg

In a medium bowl, combine the applesauce, sour cream, egg whites and molasses. Blend well. In a large bowl, mix together the flour, baking soda, salt and spices. Mix the applesauce mixture, flour mixture and the hot water together, alternating the addition of each to blend well. Lightly coat a 9" x 13" cooking pan with the spray and pour the batter into it. Put the wire rack on the lower shelf position of the rotisserie and put the gingerbread on the rack. Set the Timer for 30 minutes and cook at 425°F. Test the gingerbread by inserting a toothpick into the cake. When the cake is done, the toothpick will come out clean. If the cake is not done, resume cooking for an additional 5–10 minutes. Blend the powdered sugar and the lemon juice in a small bowl. While still warm, drizzle the gingerbread with the lemon glaze. Serves 16.

Chocolate Cheesecake

This elegant dessert is beautiful and perfect for guests.

1 c.	graham cracker crumbs
3 T.	sugar
1/4 c.	lowfat margarine
1	8 oz. pkg. fat-free cream cheese
1 c.	fat-free sour cream
1/2 c.	cocoa
1/4 c.	flour
1 t.	vanilla
1/2 t.	salt
3	egg whites
1 T.	grated semisweet chocolate
	non-stick cooking spray

NUTRITIONAL ANALYSIS

Calories:	178
Total fat:	5 g
Saturated fat:	2 g
% calories fat:	25
Carbohydrates:	26 g
Protein:	8 g
Cholesterol:	4 mg
Sodium:	398 mg

Lightly coat a 9-inch pie plate with the spray. In a small bowl, mix the cracker crumbs, sugar and margarine. Press into the bottom of the pan. In a medium bowl, blend the cream cheese, sour cream, cocoa, flour, vanilla, salt and egg whites with a mixer and beat for 3 minutes. Fold in the grated chocolate. Pour the batter over the crust. Place the wire rack on the lower shelf of the rotisserie and put the cheesecake on the rack. Set the Timer for 1 hour and bake at 300°F. Test the cake by lightly wiggling the pan. If the cake is done, the center will be firm and a knife inserted in the middle will be clean. If not, resume cooking for an additional 5–10 minutes. Cool and refrigerate overnight. Serves 10.

Black Forest Torte

A little more work, but worth it!

1/4 c.	lowfat margarine
1/4 c.	prune lekvar (puree)
3/4 c.	sugar
2	egg whites
1 t.	vanilla
2 1/4 c.	sifted cake flour
1/4 c.	cocoa
1 t.	baking soda
1/4 t.	salt
1	8 oz. lowfat plain yogurt
	non-stick cooking spray

Layers:

1 c.	cherry pie filling
1 c.	non-fat whipped topping
1 T.	grated semisweet chocolate

NUTRITIONAL ANALYSIS

Calories: 255
Total fat: 4 g
Saturated fat: 1 g
% calories fat: 13
Carbohydrates: 50 g
Protein: 4 g
Cholesterol: 1 mg
Sodium: 258 mg

Lightly coat a 9" x 13" baking pan with the cooking spray. In a medium bowl, combine the margarine, lekvar, sugar, egg whites and vanilla. Blend well. Mix together and add the flour, cocoa, baking soda and salt. Mix the sugar and egg batter with the dry ingredients and the yogurt, alternating the addition of each to blend well. Pour the batter into the pan. Place the wire rack on the lower shelf position of the rotisserie and put the cake on the rack. Set the Timer for 25–30 minutes and cook at 425°F. When done, a toothpick inserted in the middle should come out clean. If the cake is not done, resume cooking for an additional 5–10 minutes. Cool the cake for at least 30 minutes. To assemble the torte, cut the cake in half widthwise, to create two 6½" x 9" cakes . Place the bottom half on a serving plate. Cover with cherry pie filling. Put the other torte layer on top and cover with the whipped topping. Garnish with the grated chocolate. Refrigerate for 2 hours. Serves 10.

Cinnamon Oatmeal Cookies

These cookies have a chewy texture and spicy flavor.

$1/2$ c.	sugar	
$1/2$ c.	packed brown sugar	
2 T.	lowfat margarine	
$1/2$ c.	unsweetened applesauce	
1 t.	vanilla	
2	egg whites	
1 t.	baking soda	
1 t.	cinnamon	
$1/2$ t.	salt	
$2 1/2$ c.	instant rolled oats	
$1/2$ c.	flour	
	non-stick cooking spray	

NUTRITIONAL ANALYSIS

Calories:	44
Total fat:	<1 g
Saturated fat:	<1 g
% calories fat:	11
Carbohydrates:	9 g
Protein:	1 g
Cholesterol:	0 mg
Sodium:	79 mg

Lightly coat the rotisserie baking sheet with non-stick spray. In a medium bowl, combine the sugar, brown sugar, margarine, applesauce, vanilla and egg whites. Mix together and stir in the baking soda, cinnamon, salt, oats and flour. Drop the dough by rounded teaspoons onto the baking sheet. Set the Timer for 13–15 minutes and bake at 400°F. Repeat with the remaining cookie dough. Makes 3 dozen cookies.

Lowfat Chocolate Brownies

Prune lekvar, or puree, can replace the high-fat ingredients in many baking recipes. You can find it in the canned fruit section of your supermarket. You may also substitute strained prune baby food, if necessary.

1	22 oz. pkg. fudge brownie mix
1 t.	water
1 t.	vegetable oil
1/2 c.	prune lekvar
1	egg white
	non-stick cooking spray

NUTRITIONAL ANALYSIS

Calories:	245
Total fat:	6 g
Saturated fat:	1 g
% calories fat:	22
Carbohydrates:	46 g
Protein:	3 g
Cholesterol:	1 mg
Sodium:	213 mg

Lightly coat an 8" x 8" glass baking pan with the spray. Combine the brownie mix, water, oil, lekvar and egg white and blend well. Pour into the baking pan. Place the wire rack on the lower shelf position of the rotisserie and put the pan on it. Set the Timer for 25–30 minutes and bake at 400°F. Cool and cut into squares. Serves 12.

Chapter 8

The Big George Rotisserie Basic Cooking Guide

A NOTE TO THE COOK

- Your Big George Rotisserie is easy to use when you follow the step-by-step instructions in your Owner's Manual. And, when you need a quick reference for cooking, grilling and baking in the Big George Rotisserie, follow the guidelines offered below.

- Several factors contribute to the cooking time of your foods, including the weight, thickness and texture of various meats. As a result, you'll notice that recommendations for the times are often given with 5–15 minute allowances. Set your Timer for the least amount of time indicated and, after testing your food, add another 5–10 minutes, if necessary. This will help you to avoid overcooking foods unnecessarily.

■ At the end of this guide, you'll find a Big George Rotisserie cooking chart for your own notes. Use this chart to jot down your preferred cooking times for the recipes in this book or to help you organize the times and temperatures for your own recipes.

■ ■ ■

THE BIG GEORGE ROTISSERIE BASIC COOKING GUIDE

FOOD		TIMER	SELECT ELEMENTS	TEMP
BEEF				
Roast	3-4 lbs.	1½–2 hours	4	350°F
	5-6 lbs.	2–2½ hours	4	350°F
Steak	flank, 1 lb.	20–25 minutes	4	450°F
	sirloin, 4-6 oz.	20–25 minutes	4	450°F
	bone-in, 4-6 oz.	20–28 minutes	4	450°F
Kebab	1-inch piece	25–30 minutes	4	450°F
Hamburger	¼-inch thick patty	15–20 minutes	4	450°F
	½-inch thick patty	20–25 minutes	4	450°F

FOOD		TIMER	SELECT ELEMENTS	TEMP
VEAL				
Roast	3–4 lbs.	1½–2 hours	4	350°F
	5–6 lbs.	2–2½ hours	4	350°F
Cutlet	4–6 oz.	20–25 minutes	4	425°F
Chop	4–6 oz.	20–25 minutes	4	425°F
PORK				
Roast	3–4 lbs.	1½–2 hours	4	350°F
	4–5 lbs.	2–2½ hours	4	350°F
Ham, fully cooked	4–5 lbs.	1–1¼ hours	4	350°F
Ham slice, cooked	1 lb.	15 minutes	4	450°F
Chop, bone in	4–6 oz.	25–28 minutes	4	425°F
Tenderloin	4–6 oz.	20–25 minutes	4	425°F
Kebab	1-inch piece	25–30 minutes	4	450°F

FOOD		TIMER	SELECT ELEMENTS	TEMP
LAMB				
Roast	3–4 lbs.	1½–2 hours	4	350°F
	5–6 lbs.	2–2½ hours	4	350°F
Chop, bone in	4–6 oz.	15–20 minutes	4	400°F
Kebab	1-inch piece	25-30 minutes	4	400°F
POULTRY				
Turkey	14–16 lbs.	4½–5 hours	4	350°F
Turkey breast, boneless	4–5 lbs.	1½–2 hours	4	350°F
Turkeyburger	½-inch thick patty	15–20 minutes	4	450°F
Chicken, whole	3–4 lbs.	1¼–1½ hours	4	350°F
	5–6 lbs.	1½–2 hours	4	350°F

FOOD		TIMER	SELECT ELEMENTS	TEMP
Chicken breast, boneless	4–6 oz.	15–20 minutes	4	425°F
Chicken, kebab	1-inch piece	15–20 minutes	4	425°F
Game Hen	1–1½ lbs.	25–30 minutes	4	400°F
Duckling	4–5 lbs.	1¾–2 hours	4	400°F
FISH & SHELLFISH				
Steak	4–6 oz., ¾-inch thick	15–20 minutes	4	450°F
Kebab	1-inch piece	15–20 minutes	4	450°F
Lean Fillet	4–6 oz., ½-inch thick	15–18 minutes	4	450°F
Shrimp, raw, peeled	Large/Jumbo	15–20 minutes	4	450°F

FOOD		TIMER	SELECT ELEMENTS	TEMP
VEGETABLES/FRUITS				
Vegetable Kebab	2-inch piece	25–30 minutes	4	450°F
AirBake Vegetable	½-inch piece	35–45 minutes	4	425°F
Fruit Kebab	1-inch piece	15–20 minutes	4	425°F
Fruit	halves	15–20 minutes	4	425°F
BAKED FOODS				
Casserole	9" x 13" pan	35–45 minutes	4	425°F
Cornbread	9" x 13" pan	25–30 minutes	4	425°F
Muffins	12-cup muffin pan	15–18 minutes	4	425°F
Breadsticks	baking sheet	20–25 minutes	4	450°F
Cheesecake	9" pie pan	1–1¼ hours	3	300°F
Cookies	baking sheet	10–12 minutes	4	400°F

ROTISSERIE COOKING: PERSONAL NOTES

FOOD	TIMER	SELECT ELEMENTS	TEMP

FOOD	TIMER	SELECT ELEMENTS	TEMP

Glossary

Acid reaction. Marinades typically include acids in the form of juice or vinegar to break down the connective meat tissue and act as a tenderizer. These acids react when left in contact with aluminum, therefore it's best to use glass or plastic containers to mix and marinate.

Adjustable Basket. Your rotisserie includes an adjustable basket for cooking foods unsuitable for the rotisserie bar, such as steaks and chops. Refer to the Owner's Manual for complete instructions on the use and care of this accessory.

Allspice. This aromatic spice comes from the West Indian myrtle tree.

Au jus. A French word used to describe the thin beef broth that accompanies roasts.

Baking Sheet. Your rotisserie includes a baking sheet that allows you to bake in the rotisserie oven. Refer to the Owner's Manual for complete instructions on the use and care of this accessory.

Balsamic vinegar. The balsam tree contributes the aromatic taste of this vinegar.

Cajun. This term refers to the very spicy mix of herbs and flavors that has its origins in Louisiana.

Calorie. A unit of measure that has an energy-producing value. People who are modifying their eating habits typically try to consume fewer calories in their foods, as well as burn more calories through exercise.

Carbohydrate. Foods that contain compounds of carbon, hydrogen and oxygen. These foods include sugars and starches.

Chili powder. This very spicy powder is made from finely ground red peppers.

Cilantro. This Mexican parsley has a more defined flavor than its American counterpart. It flavors marinades and sauces exceptionally well.

Contamination. When cooking meats, fish and poultry, bacteria can easily spread and contaminate, or render unusable, another food product. Use a separate cutting board and utensils for raw meats and avoid re-using dishcloths after you've handled meats and washed your hands.

Coriander. From the carrot family, this aromatic herb has been used since ancient days to flavor meats.

Crostini. Italian bread rounds perfect for small appetizers.

Cumin. From the carrot family, this spicy herb is used in various Italian and Mexican dishes to add distinctive flavor.

Dijon mustard. Usually distilled with white wine and spices, this mustard is more mild and has less "bite" than typical yellow mustard.

Dressed. A fish is "dressed" when it has the head, tail and gills removed and is eviscerated.

Entrée. This French word meaning "the act of entering" has been adapted to more than one definition over the past two centuries. In England, the word is used to describe the dish served before the roast and in America the word is used to describe the main dish of the meal.

Fillet. The term "fillet" is used to describe either the tenderloin of meat or a boneless piece of fish.

Five-spice powder. An oriental blend of herbs and spices.

Gram. This metric unit is used for fat measurement. It is equivalent to .035 ounces.

Hoisin sauce. This rich and smooth oriental sauce is commonly used to add bold flavor to meats and marinades.

Kebab. Cubes of meat usually marinated and grilled with vegetables.

Lentils. Similar to beans, these flat seeds are a valuable source of carbohydrates.

Linguine. Long, flat and fairly thin pasta noodles.

Liquid egg product. Commercial egg substitutes have no fat, no cholesterol and can typically be found in the refrigerated section of the dairy case in your supermarket.

Liquid smoke. These small bottles of smoke-flavored seasoning can be found in the spice and flavoring section of your supermarket.

Lowfat. This term refers to any food that has a proportionately lower number of fat grams than most foods commonly prepared and eaten. The U.S. Department of Agriculture has standards for any commercial food product before the term, "lowfat" can be advertised or applied.

Marbled. A cut of meat has fat that is variegated throughout and the term, "marbled" or "marbling" refers to that fat. Typically, the more marbling a cut of meat contains, the more fat it will also have overall.

Marinade. An acid-based sauce used to infuse meats, poultry and fish with flavor. This can also be a tenderizing process as the acid breaks down the connective tissue in meats.

Obesity. This condition refers to extreme and excessive fat on the human body.

Pesto. An Italian basil sauce that pairs well with meats and poultry. It is oftentimes accompanied by pine nuts.

Polenta. A favorite Italian meal accompaniment, polenta is a thick, herb-flavored cornmeal patty.

Prune lekvar. Prune puree or "lekvar," as it is commonly called, is an excellent substitute for fat in baked goods. The moist and mild-flavored properties of the prunes create tender muffins, cakes and cookies. Applesauce can also be used in this manner.

Reduced-fat. A food that has had some of the fat removed but is not considered "lowfat," by U.S. Department of Agriculture standards. Read the labels carefully to determine the actual fat gram count when selecting reduced-fat foods, as some may still have high amounts.

Rice wine vinegar. This white oriental vinegar is less acidic than cider vinegar and can be found in the condiment section of your supermarket.

Rigatoni. Medium-sized tubes of pasta that are especially good in salads and soups.

Risotto. This Italian word refers to a rice dish that is slightly more moist than typical American rice and often has herbs, spices or mushrooms as ingredients.

Roasted Veggie/Air Bake Basket. Your rotisserie includes this unique basket for cooking foods such as potatoes and vegetables without any added oils or fat. Refer to the Owner's Manual for complete instructions on the use and care of this accessory.

Rotisserie. A method of cooking meat that involves the rotation of the meat on a bar or spit over flame or heating elements. Fat drips away from the meat in this method of cooking and the juices of the meat are seared inside, resulting in tenderness and a lower fat content overall.

Rotisserie Bar. This bar holds the meat or poultry and facilitates turning while the food cooks. Food should always be properly centered on the bar for best results. Refer to the Owner's Manual for complete instructions on the use and care of this accessory.

Rotisserie Timer. Your rotisserie contains an electronic timer to pre-select the cooking time. There are many features of the timer and each is referenced in the Owner's Manual.

Rub. A mixture of spices and herbs that are pressed into the meat, fish or poultry prior to cooking. Rubs do not contain oil or juices and can be stored in the refrigerator for up to one month.

Sage. A favorite herb used with poultry, sage actually comes from the mint family.

Savory. A European mint used in aromatic cooking. This herb is normally used to develop the flavor of beef.

Tenderize. The overall tenderness of a cut of beef or pork varies widely. Usually the most tender meats also contain the most fat. In order to tenderize and accent the flavor of a lower-fat cut of meat, a marinade can be used. The marinade infuses a portion of the meat and tenderizes it without adding additional fat.

Vermicelli. Long, very thin pasta noodles similar to spaghetti.

Ziti. Pasta shaped into thin, cylindrical tubes. This pasta is used in casseroles and salads.

Index

George Foreman Grilling Machines

For information or to order any of these other products
in the George Foreman "family," call Salton at

1-800-233-9054

or visit our website:
http//www.salton-maxim.com
or e-mail us at Salton@Saltonusa.com

George Foreman Party Grill

George Foreman Grill Away Grill Pans